MATH

101 Things Every KINDERGARTNER Should Know About MATH

Peg Hall
Consultant: Susan A. Miller, Ed.D.

active minds®

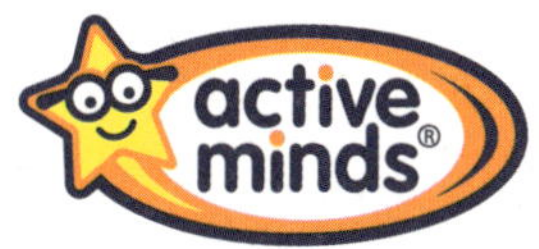

Peg Hall has written numerous teacher guides and student activity books, as well as fiction and nonfiction books for children. She has worked as a reading resource teacher, an editor, and an education consultant. Ms. Hall currently works as a freelance writer from her home in coastal Massachusetts.

Susan A. Miller, Ed.D., is a Professor Emerita of Early Childhood Education at Kutztown University of Pennsylvania. She is a columnist for Scholastic's *Early Childhood Today* and *Parent & Child* magazines. She has been the consultant or writer for numerous books, including *My First Dictionary, Circle Time Activities, Problem Solving Kids,* and *Games, Giggles, and Giant Steps.* Dr. Miller is a frequent presenter at the National Association for the Education of Young Children Conferences and the Association for Childhood Education International Conferences.

Illustrations by **George Ulrich.**

Louis Weber, CEO
Publications International, Ltd.
7373 North Cicero Avenue
Lincolnwood, Illinois 60712

www.myactiveminds.com

ISBN-13: 978-1-4127-1233-0
ISBN-10: 1-4127-1233-5

Manufactured in China.

8 7 6 5 4 3 2 1

Contents

Add Some Fun to Math

Dear Parents:

Starting school is an exciting time for kindergartners. They are ready for new challenges, such as learning to read, write, and make sense of numbers. They seem to want to know more about everything! Of course you want to give your child that special head start that is so important. This workbook will help your child learn the basic skills of a vast array of math concepts and processes—skills your child will build on in future learning.

Inside this workbook, children will find 101 fun-filled math activities right at their fingertips. Each activity focuses on a different skill and provides your child with plenty of opportunity to practice that skill. The activities are arranged in order of difficulty, beginning with the most basic skills in order to build your child's confidence as he or she goes along. They'll feel a real sense of accomplishment as they complete each page.

Every activity is clearly labeled with the skill being taught. You will find skill keys written especially for you, the parent, at the bottom of each activity page. These skill keys give you information about what your child is learning. Also, suggestions are provided for additional hands-on activities you may choose to do with your child. These offer fun, enjoyable opportunities to reinforce the skill being taught.

Children learn in a variety of ways. They are sure to appreciate the bright, exciting illustrations in this workbook. The pictures are not just fun—they also help visual learners develop their math skills by giving them something to relate to. Children may also like to touch and trace the numbers and pictures and say them out loud. Each method can be an important aid in your child's learning process.

Your child can tackle some of the activities independently; in other cases you will need to read the directions for your child before he or she can complete the exercise. Each activity should be fun and enough of a challenge that it will be exciting for your child. Be patient and support your child in positive ways. Let them know it's all right to take a guess or pull back if they're unsure. And, of course, celebrate their successes with them. Learning should be an exciting and positive experience for everyone. Enjoy your time together as your child enhances his or her kindergarten math skills.

Give a Dog a Bone!

These dogs are hungry! Draw lines to give every dog a bone.

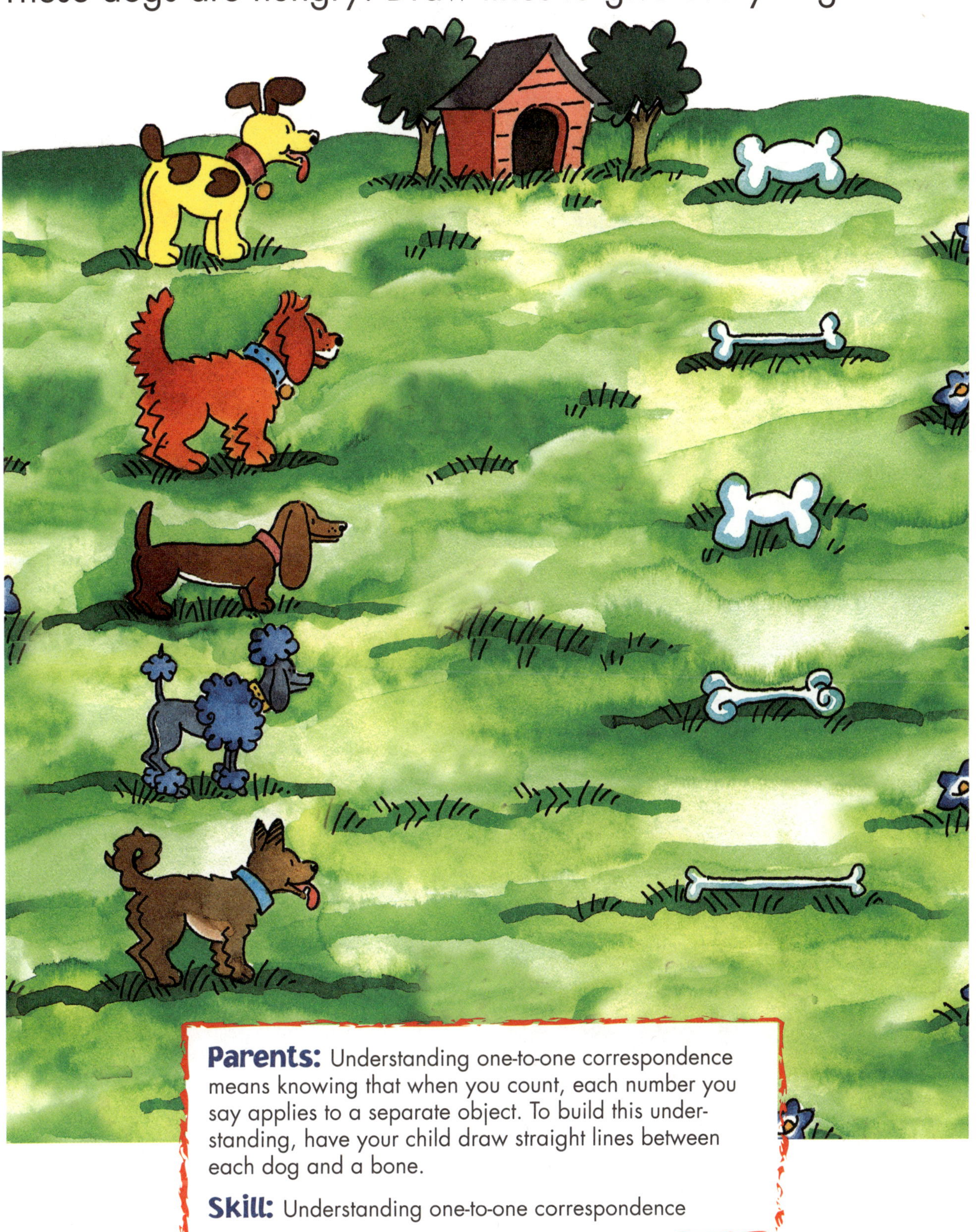

Parents: Understanding one-to-one correspondence means knowing that when you count, each number you say applies to a separate object. To build this understanding, have your child draw straight lines between each dog and a bone.

Skill: Understanding one-to-one correspondence

Answers will vary.

Toy Time

Count the toys. Draw a line through each toy as you count it.

Skill: Rote counting

The Number Train

Draw a line through the numbers on the train's cars. Read the numbers as the train moves along the track.

Skill: Reading numbers 1 through 10

Number Fun

Count how many steps the bird took. Trace the numbers on the bottom of the page. Then write them all by yourself!

1 2 3 4 5

1 2 3 4 5

____ ____ ____ ____ ____

Parents: Help your child follow the arrows to form each numeral correctly. For extra practice with number recognition, say a number from 1–10 and have your child find the bird footprint with that number.

Skill: Writing numbers 1–10

Answers on page 122.

Fun with Number 1!

Trace the number 1. Practice writing it again.

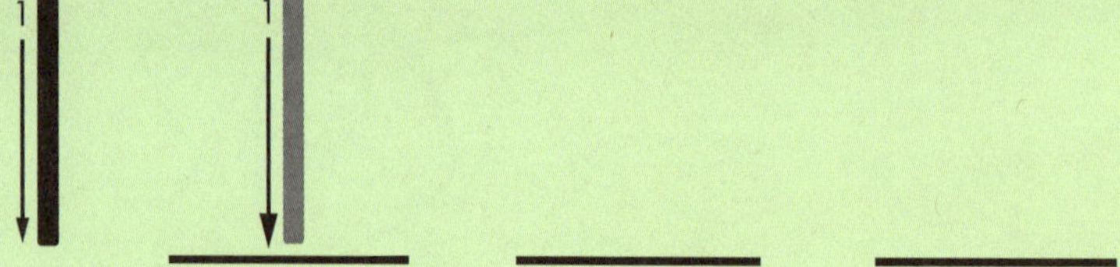

Count 1 caterpillar. Write the number.

Feed the caterpillar! Draw 1 leaf.

Skill: Understanding the value of 1

Answers on page 122.

Who's for 2?

Trace the number 2. Practice writing it again.

Count 2 anteaters. Write the number.

Feed the anteaters! Draw 2 ants.

Skill: Understanding the value of 2

Answers on page 122.

Come and See the Number 3!

Trace the number 3. Practice writing it again.

Count 3 spiders. Write the number.

Feed the spiders! Draw 3 flies.

Skill: Understanding the value of 3

Answers on page 122.

Roar for 4!

Trace the number 4. Practice writing it again.

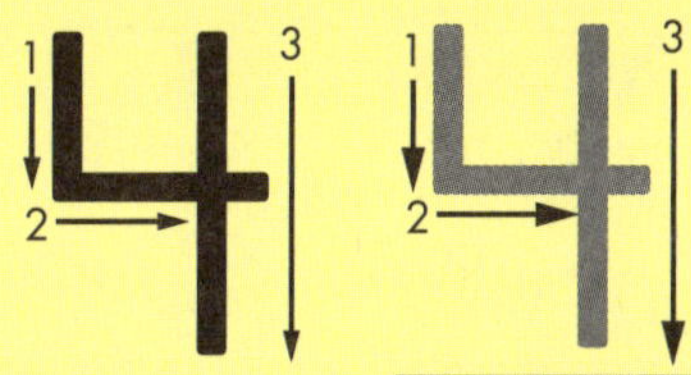

Count 4 bears. Write the number.

Feed the bears! Draw 4 fish.

Skill: Understanding the value of 4

Answers on page 122.

Dive for 5!

Trace the number 5. Practice writing it again.

Count 5 seagulls. Write the number.

Feed the seagulls! Draw 5 little fish.

Skill: Understanding the value of 5

Answers on page 122.

6 Doing Tricks!

Trace the number 6. Practice writing it again.

Count 6 monkeys. Write the number.

Feed the monkeys! Draw 6 bananas.

Skill: Understanding the value of 6

Answers on page 122.

Hippety-Hop to 7!

Trace the number 7. Practice writing it again.

Count 7 rabbits. Write the number.

Feed the rabbits! Draw 7 carrots.

Skill: Understanding the value of 7

Answers on page 122.

Number 8 Is Really Great!

Trace the number 8. Practice writing it again.

Count 8 bees. Write the number.

Feed the bees! Draw 8 flowers.

Skill: Understanding the value of 8

Answers on page 122.

Doing Fine with Number 9!

Trace the number 9. Practice writing it again.

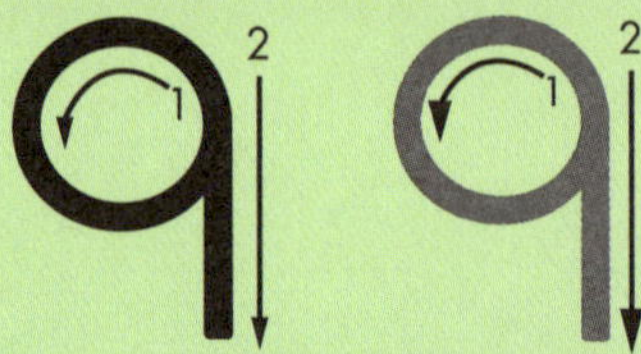

Count 9 squirrels. Write the number.

Feed the squirrels! Draw 9 nuts.

Skill: Understanding the value of 9

Answers on page 122.

Hooray for 10!

Trace the number 10. Practice writing it again.

10 10 ___ ___

Count 10 birds. Write the number.

Feed the birds! Draw 10 worms.

Skill: Understanding the value of 10

Answers on page 122.

Picnic Packing

Here is 1 big picnic basket. Trace the 1.

Count the things that go in the basket. Write the numbers.

Skill: Reviewing the value of numbers 1–10

Answers on page 123.

Road Trip

What is coming down the road? Connect the dots from 1 to 10 to see.

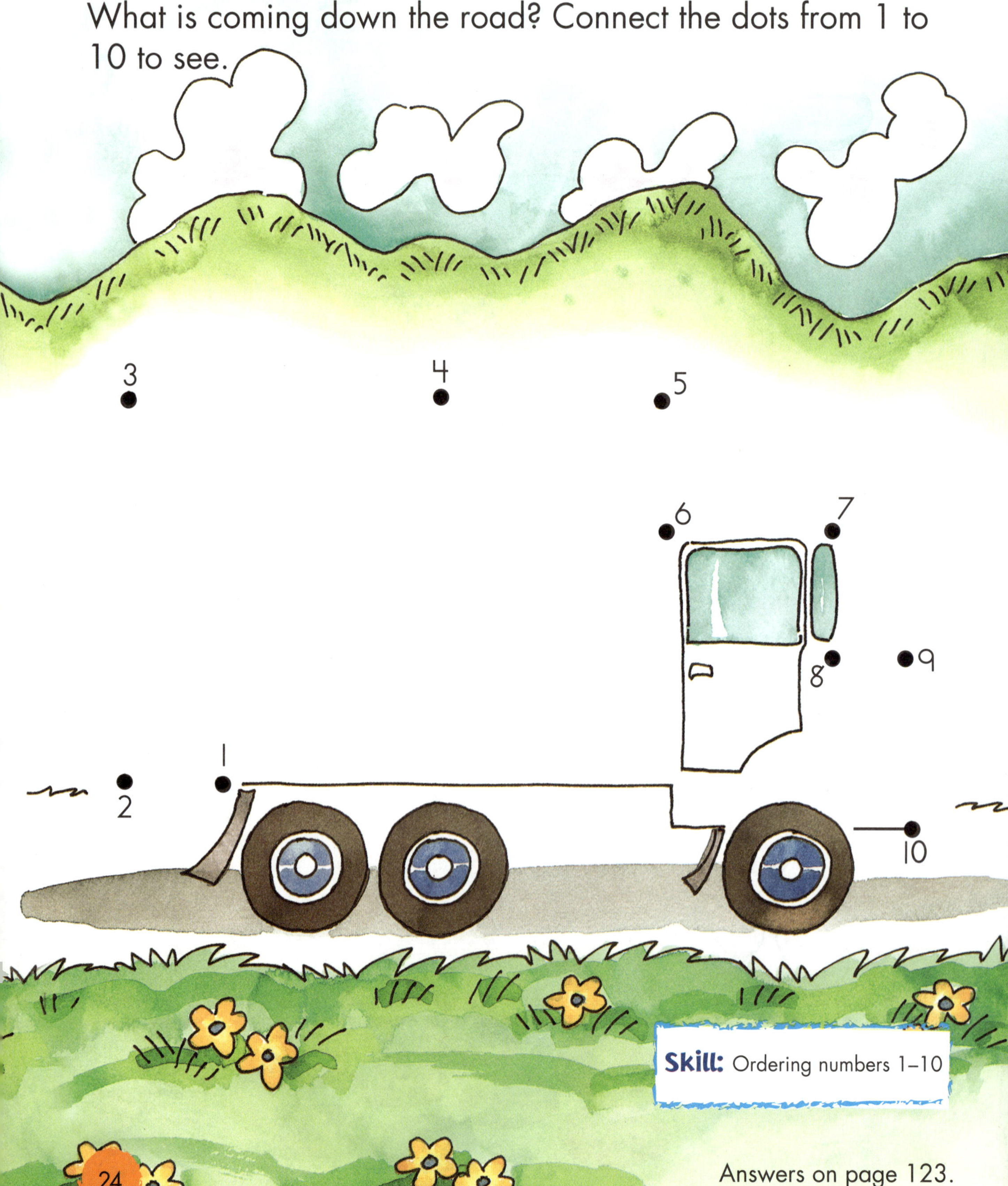

Skill: Ordering numbers 1–10

Answers on page 123.

A Line of Numbers

These numbers are all in a line. Read the numbers out loud.

1 2 3 4 5 6 7 8 9 10

Some numbers are missing from this fence! Write the missing numbers.

Write the numbers that are missing from this fence.

Skill: Locating numbers on a number line

Answers on page 123.

Blast Off!

Help the rocket go into space. Count backward from 10 to 1. Then try writing the numbers after you say them.

Skill: Counting backward from 10

Answers on page 123.

Words for Numbers

You can read number words. Read to find out how many things to draw.

1 one 

Draw one rocket.

2 two 

Draw two raindrops.

3 three

Draw three moons.

4 four

Draw four suns.

5 five

Draw five clouds.

Skill: Recognizing number words 1–5

Answers on page 123.

Number Word Jungle

Here are more numbers and number words.

6	7	8	9	10
six	seven	eight	nine	ten

Count the animals. Circle the number word that tells how many.

eight nine

nine ten

Skill: Recognizing number words 6–10

Answers on page 123.

Getting Together

Some things go together.

This is a set of fruits. Why do you think they go together?

Cross out the thing that is not a toy.

Cross out the thing that is not an animal.

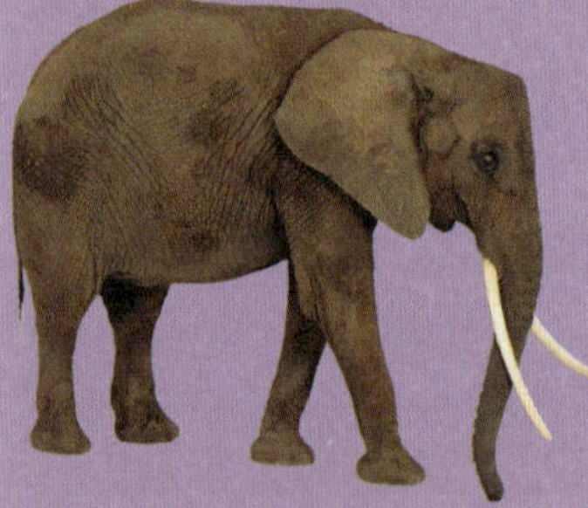

Cross out the thing that is not a flower.

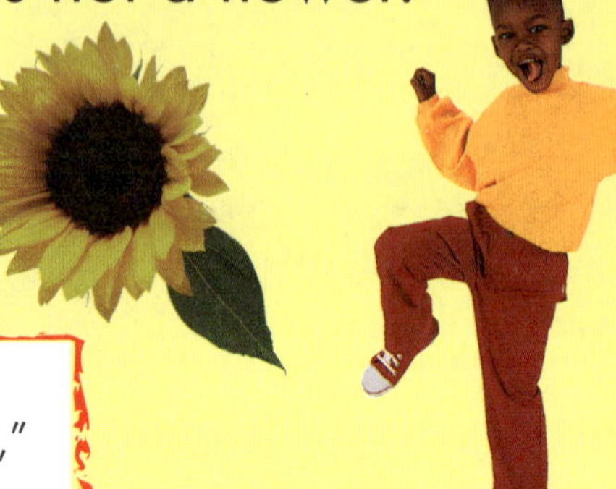

Parents: Help your child become familiar with the concept of sets. Ask your child to make "a set of 3 balls," "a set of red blocks," and so on.

Skill: Understanding the concept of sets

Answers on page 123.

Buggy Sets

Look at the sets. Count the number of bugs in each set. Draw a line to the number that matches how many bugs are in each set.

Skill: Matching numerals to sets

Answers on page 123.

Making Sets

Count the marbles to make sets.

Count 10 marbles. Put an X through each marble as you count to 10. Circle the set of 10.

Count 5 marbles. Put an X through each marble as you count to 5. Circle the set of 5.

Count 6 marbles. Put an X through each marble as you count to 6. Circle the set of 6.

Count 4 marbles. Put an X through each marble as you count to 4. Circle the set of 4.

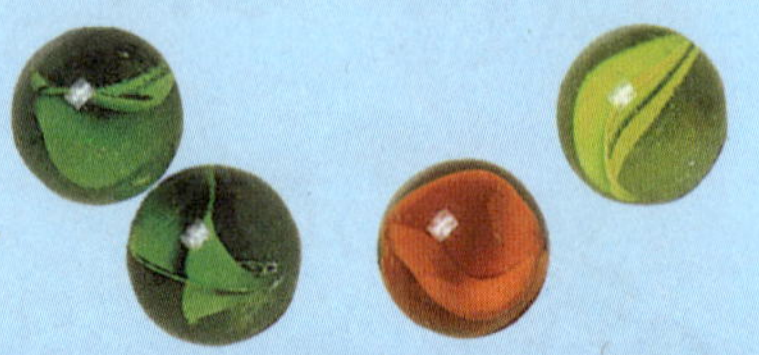

Count 2 marbles. Put an X through each marble as you count to 2. Circle the set of 2.

Count 8 marbles. Put an X through each marble as you count to 8. Circle the set of 8.

Skill: Making sets of objects

Answers will vary.

Make Some More!

Draw 1 more sock. Count how many all together

Draw 2 more hats. Count how many all together.

Draw 3 more boots. Count how many all together

Circle the set that has more snow pants.

Parents: Understanding the concept of more is essential to learning how to add. Ask your child questions such as "Who has more cookies?" Then count them. Ask the child to "add 1 more" to a set of objects. Then ask how many there are in the set.

Skill: Understanding the concept of more

Answers on page 123.

Fewer at the Frog Pond

Count the frogs.

3 frogs

One frog hopped away!

2 frogs

Count the fish in each pond. Circle the set that has fewer fish.

Count the worms in the dirt. Circle the set that has fewer worms.

Count the turtles on each rock. Circle the set that has fewer turtles.

Parents: Understanding the concept of fewer is essential to learning how to subtract. Ask questions like "Who has fewer marbles?" or "Which pile has fewer pennies?"

Skill: Understanding the concept of fewer

Answers on page 123.

Animals Above, Below, and On

Where is the duck? Above, below, or on the boat?

Skill: Understanding positional words: above, below, and on

Answers on page 123.

Animals Beside and Between

Where is the scorpion?

beside

between

Circle the word that tells where the bird is standing.

beside between

beside between

Circle the word that tells where the rabbit is standing.

beside between

beside between

Skill: Understanding positional words: beside and between

Answers on page 123.

Finish the Picture

Draw a sun above the house. Draw a window beside the door. Draw a rabbit below the house. Draw a bird on the roof. Draw a boy between the trees.

Parents: Read the directions, one sentence at a time, to your child. Have him or her draw each object in the correct position.

Skill: Placing objects in specified positions

Answers on page 123.

Looking at Lines

Lines can be straight or curved.

straight

curved

Put an X on the straight lines.

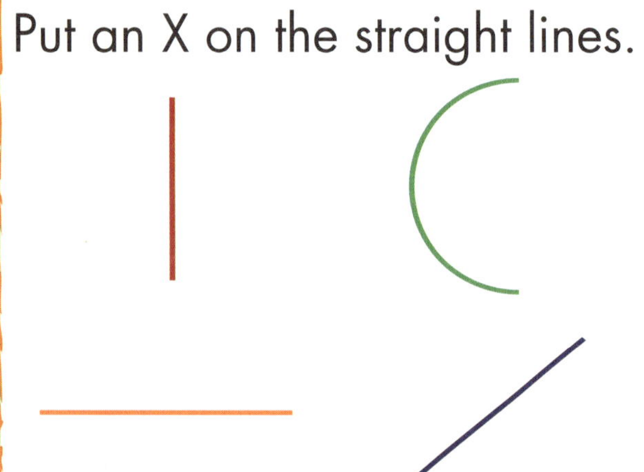

Put an X on the curved lines.

Circle the things that have straight lines.

Circle the things that have curved lines.

Skill: Recognizing curved and straight lines

Answers on page 123.

What Is a Circle?

A circle is round. A circle is made with a curved line.
Draw your own circles.

Find the circles. Color them **red.** Write how many circles you see. ______

Skill: Recognizing circles

Answers on page 124.

What Is a Square?

A square has 4 sides that are equal. A square is made with straight lines. Draw your own squares.

Find the squares. Color them **green.** Write how many squares you see. ______

Skill: Recognizing squares

Answers on page 124.

What Is a Triangle?

A triangle has 3 sides. A triangle is made with 3 straight lines. Draw your own triangles.

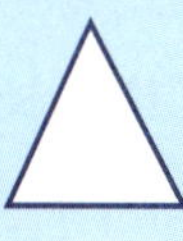

Find the triangles. Color them **yellow.** Write how many triangles you see. ______

Skill: Recognizing triangles

Answers on page 124.

What Is a Rectangle?

A rectangle has 4 sides. A rectangle is made with 4 straight lines. The opposite sides are equal in length. Draw your own rectangles.

Find the rectangles. Color them **blue.** Write how many rectangles you see. ______

Skill: Recognizing rectangles

Answers on page 124.

Shape Hunt

Shapes are everywhere! Just look around.

Put an X on the things that are circles.

Put an X on the things that are squares.

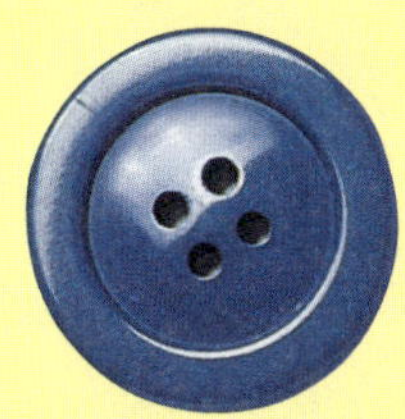

Put an X on the things that are triangles.

Put an X on the things that are rectangles.

Parents: Go on a shape hunt with your child. Look around inside and outside your home for objects that are shaped like circles, squares, triangles, and rectangles.

Skill: Recognizing geometric shapes in real life

Answers on page 124.

Making Shapes

Trace the circle.

Trace the square.

Draw a circle.

Draw a square.

Trace the dotted shapes to finish the pictures.

Skill: Drawing circles and squares

Answers on page 124.

More Shapes to Make

Trace the triangle.

Trace the rectangle.

Draw a triangle.

Draw a rectangle.

Trace the dotted shapes to finish the pictures.

Skill: Drawing triangles and rectangles

Answers on page 124.

Find the Shapes

Color the circles **yellow.** Color the squares **blue.**
Color the triangles **red.**
Color the rectangles **green.**

Skill: Reviewing geometric shapes

Answers on page 124.

How Long?

How long is the stick? Count the paper clips to measure.

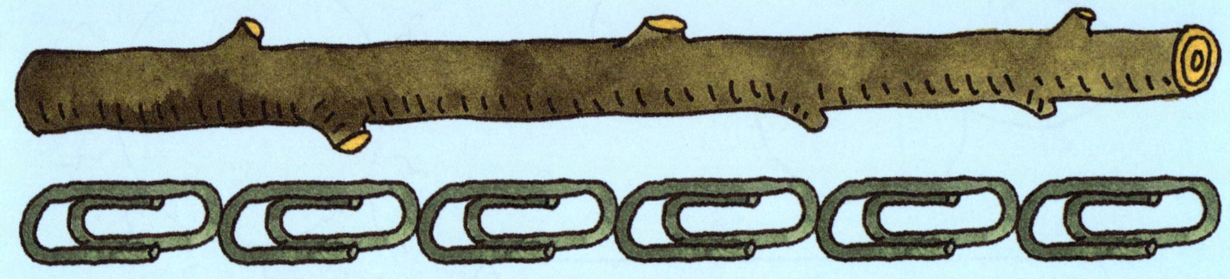

The stick is 6 paper clips long.

How long is the snake? Count the paper clips to measure.

The snake is _____ paper clips long.

How long is the book? Count the paper clips to measure.

The book is _____ paper clips long.

Parents: Build the concept of measurement by having your child lay paper clips end to end to measure a toy, book, or table. Help your child experiment with other nonstandard measurements, such as using pencils or fingers to measure the length of an object.

Skill: Measuring with nonstandard units

Answers on page 124.

Big and Little

Some things are big.

Some things are little.

Circle something big.

Circle something little.

Skill: Recognizing big and little objects

Answers on page 124.

Long and Short

Some animals are long.

Some animals are short.

Circle the word that describes the animal's tail.

long short

long short

long short

long short

Draw a long tail on the horse.

Draw a short tail on the rabbit.

Skill: Recognizing long and short objects

Answers on page 124.

Tall and Short

Draw a short flower beside the tall flower.

Draw a tall cup beside the short cup.

Draw a tall hill beside the short hill.

Skill: Recognizing tall and short objects

Answers will vary.

Light and Heavy

light heavy

Circle something light.

Circle something heavy.

Draw something light on the red side. Draw something heavy on the green side.

Skill: Recognizing light and heavy objects

Answers on page 124.

Think About Size

Parents: Read each direction to your child, and have him or her mark the answer.

Skill: Comparing objects by size

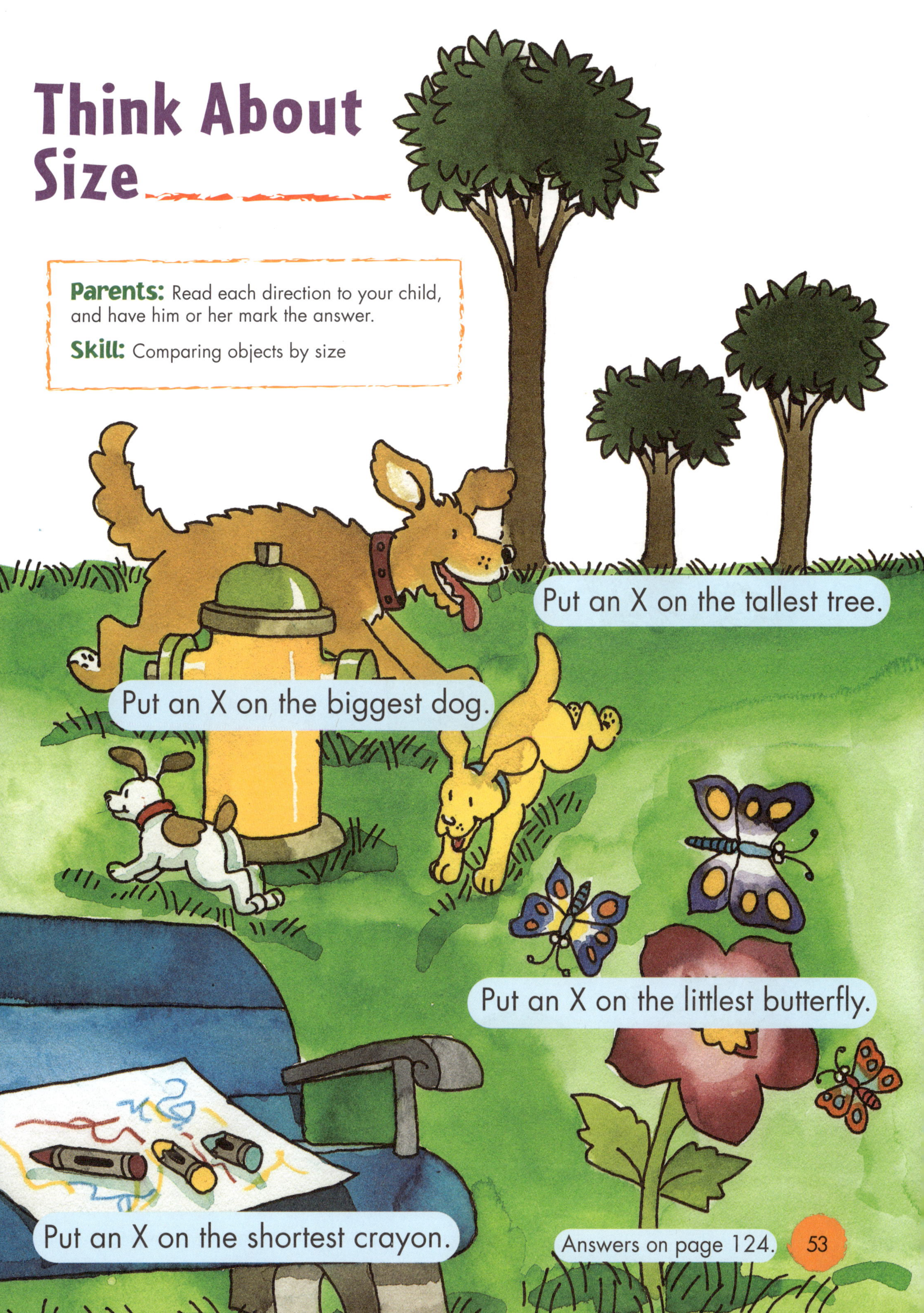

Answers on page 124.

Full and Empty

full empty

Circle the things that are full. Put an X on the things that are empty.

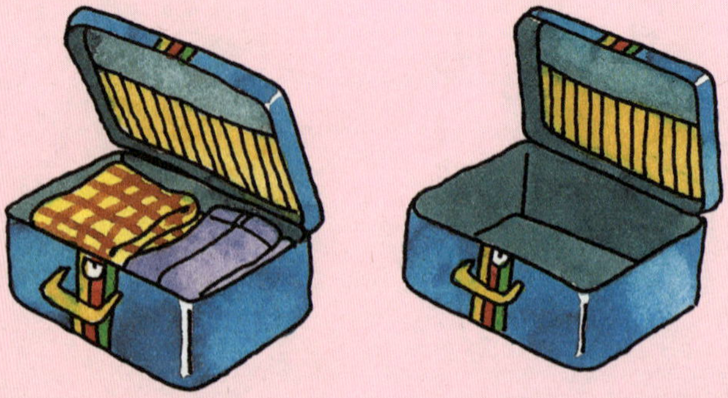

Skill: Recognizing full and empty objects

Answers on page 124.

Color and Shape Patterns

Look at the top pattern. Color the shapes below to copy the patterns.

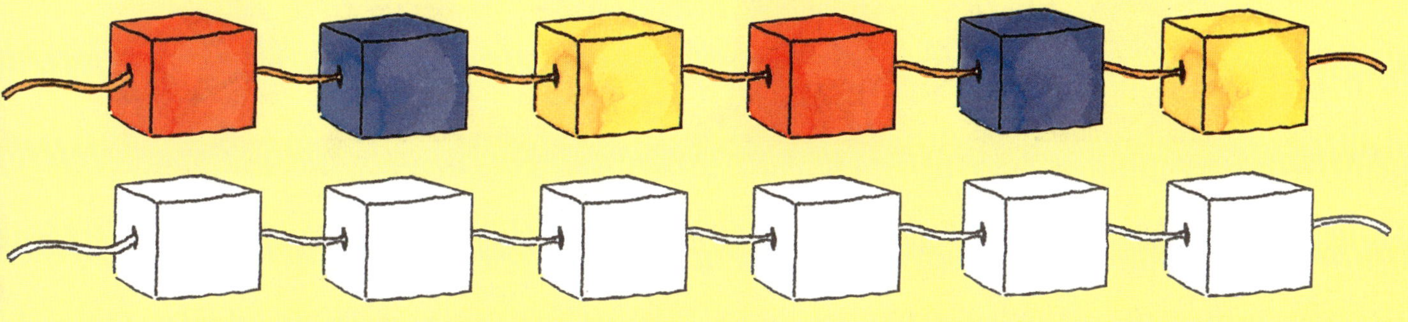

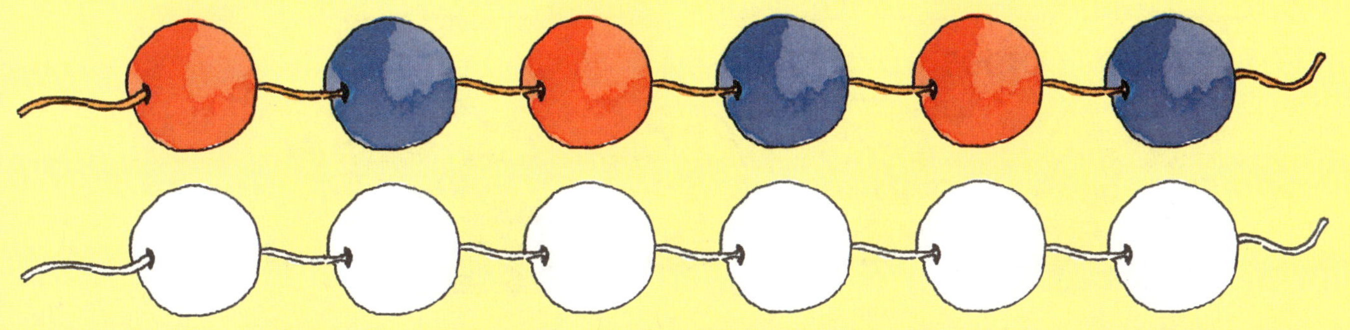

Parents: Encourage your child to replicate patterns at home using household objects such as socks and silverware.

Skill: Recognizing and reproducing patterns

Answers on page 125.

What Comes Next?

Look at the patterns. Draw what comes next.

Draw what comes next.

Draw what comes next.

Write what comes next.

1 2 3 1 2 3 1

Draw what comes next.

4 3 2 1 4 3 2

Skill: Extending patterns

Answers on page 125.

Before and After at the Zoo

The monkey had a banana <u>before</u> he ate it.
The banana was gone <u>after</u> the monkey ate it.

before

after

Draw lines to match the words to the pictures.

before after before after

Skill: Understanding before and after

Answers on page 125.

A Bunch of Birds

Touch the birds as you count them. Put a line under each number as you count from 1 to 20.

Skill: Counting by 1s to 20; reading numbers 1 through 20

A Number Party

Can you count how many presents Marie received for her birthday? Trace the numbers. Now write the numbers on the lines.

1 ____

2 ____

3 ____

4 ____

5 ____

6 ____

7 ____

8 ____

9 ____

10 ____

Parents: Help your child follow the arrows to form each numeral correctly. For extra practice with number recognition, say a number from 1 to 20 and have your child find the gift with that number.

Skill: Writing numbers 1 to 20

Answers on page 125.

Come to the 11 Party!

Trace the number 11. Practice writing it again.

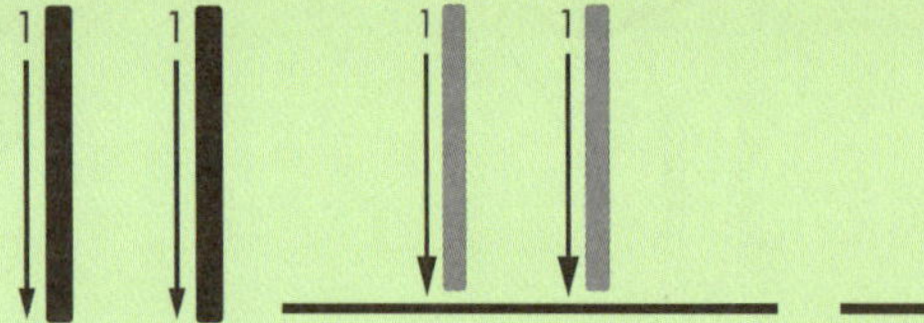

Count 11 cupcakes. Write the number.

Draw 11 birthday candles for the cupcakes.

Skill: Understanding the value of 11

Answers on page 125.

12 Party Plates

Trace the number 12. Practice writing it again.

Count 12 party plates. Write the number.

Draw 12 scoops of ice cream for the plates.

Skill: Understanding the value of 12

Answers on page 125.

13 Candles

Trace the number 13. Practice writing it again.

13 13 ______ ______ ______

Count 13 candles. Write the number.

______

Draw 13 pieces of cake for the candles.

Skill: Understanding the value of 13

Answers on page 125.

14 Great Gifts

Trace the number 14. Practice writing it again.

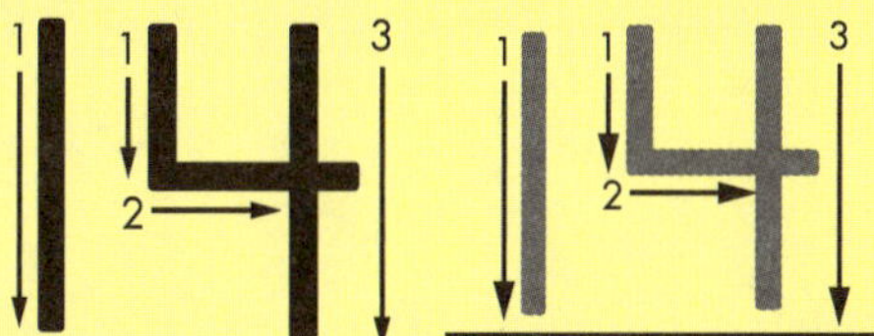

Count 14 gifts. Write the number.

       ______

Draw 14 bows for the presents.

Skill: Understanding the value of 14

Answers on page 125.

15 Pretzels

Trace the number 15. Practice writing it again.

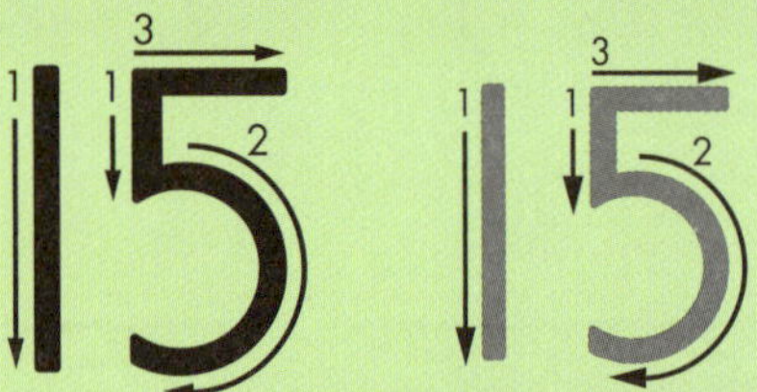

Count 15 pretzels. Write the number.

Draw 15 blobs of mustard for the pretzels.

Skill: Understanding the value of 15

Answers on page 125.

16 Kids

Trace the number 16. Practice writing it again.

16 16 ______ ______ ______

Count 16 kids. Write the number.

______

Draw 16 balloons for the kids.

Skill: Understanding the value of 16

Answers on page 125.

17 Birthday Cards

Trace the number 17. Practice writing it again.

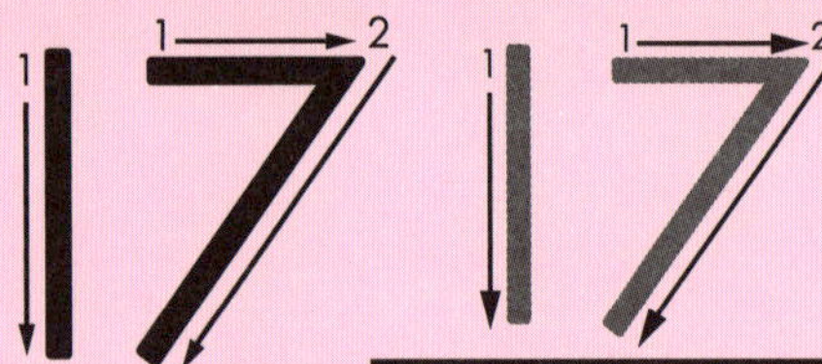

Count 17 birthday cards. Write the number.

Draw 17 stamps for the envelopes.

Skill: Understanding the value of 17

Answers on page 125.

18 Balloons

Trace the number 18. Practice writing it again.

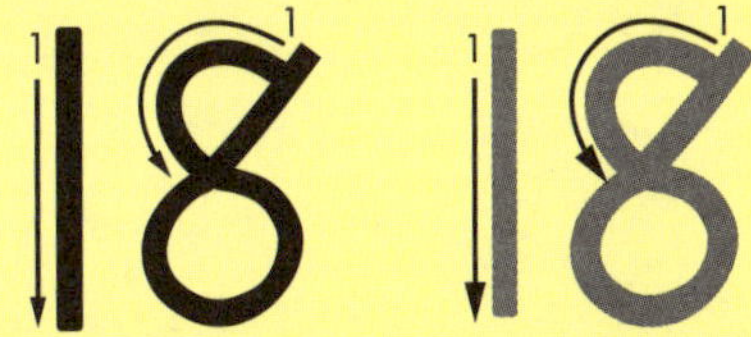

Count 18 balloons. Write the number.

Draw 18 curvy pieces of string for the balloons.

Skill: Understanding the value of 18

Answers on page 125.

19 Party Hats

Trace the number 19. Practice writing it again.

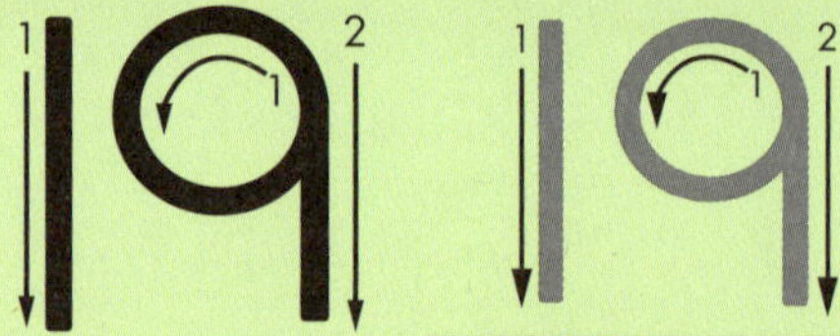

Count 19 hats. Write the number.

Draw 19 pom-poms for the hats.

Skill: Understanding the value of 19

Answers on page 125.

20 Treats

Trace the number 20. Practice writing it again.

20 20

Count 20 lollipops. Write the number.

Draw 20 sticks for the lollipops.

Skill: Understanding the value of 20

Answers on page 125.

What Is in the Garden?

Connect the dots from 1 to 20. Color what is flying in the garden.

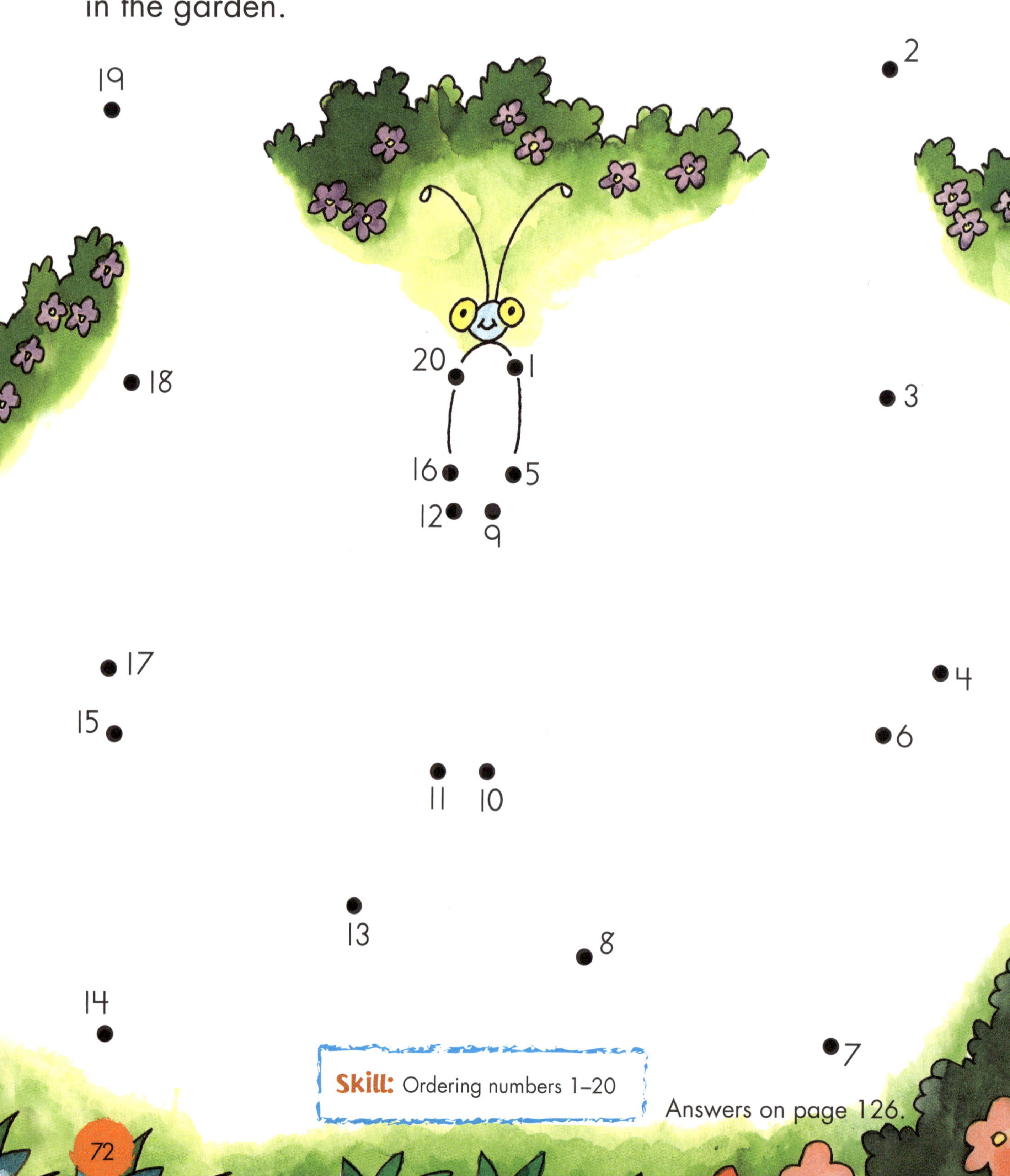

Skill: Ordering numbers 1–20

Answers on page 126.

Take a Guess!

Look at the bags. Guess how many toys are inside. Write this guess. (This is called <u>estimating.</u>)

	Guess	Count
	______	______
	______	______
	______	______

Parents: Have your child look at the pictures quickly and guess how many without taking time to count. Give your child more practice with estimating by asking him or her to guess how many books are on a shelf or how many potatoes are in a bag. Together, count to check the estimates.

Skill: Estimating quantities to 20

Answers on page 126.

Numbers on Parade

Touch each little elephant in the parade above. Say the number out loud. Touch each big elephant in the parade below. Say the number out loud. Write the number on the line.

21

22

23

24

25

26

Parents: Help your child learn larger numbers by saying a number from 21 to 31 and having your child point to the appropriate big elephant. Have your child count out loud from 1 to 31 without looking at the pages.

Skill: Reading and writing numbers 21 to 31

31

30 ______

29 ______

28 ______

27 ______

______

Answers on page 126.

Who Is Hiding?

Who is hiding in the swamp? Connect the dots from 1 to 31 to find out. Then color the swamp creature.

31 1 30 26 27 29 25 28 2 24 3 5 21 20 4 7 6 22 23 19 18 9 8 10 11 13 14 12 17 15 16

Skill: Ordering numbers to 31

Answers on page 126.

Many Months

A year has 12 months. Can you say the names of the months in order? Use these birthday balloons to help you.

Circle the month of your birthday.

Put an X on the month that comes before your birthday.

Put a ✓ on the month that comes after your birthday.

Put a ☐ around a family member's birthday month.

Parents: Help your child read the names of the months and the questions that follow, or read the page aloud to your child. Ask questions such as, "Can you name (or point to) the month that it is now?"

Skill: Naming months in order

Answers will vary.

Willy's Week

A week has 7 days. Say the days of the week in order. Use the pictures to help you read. What will Willy do each day of the week?

Sunday — Have a picnic.

Monday — Play ball.

Tuesday

Go swimming.

Wednesday

Play with toys.

Thursday — Go to the park.

Friday — Wash the dog.

Saturday

Go for a ride.

Circle the day that comes before Tuesday.

Saturday Monday

Circle the day that comes before Friday.

Thursday Sunday

Circle the day that comes after Saturday.

Sunday Tuesday

Circle the day that comes after Tuesday.

Friday Wednesday

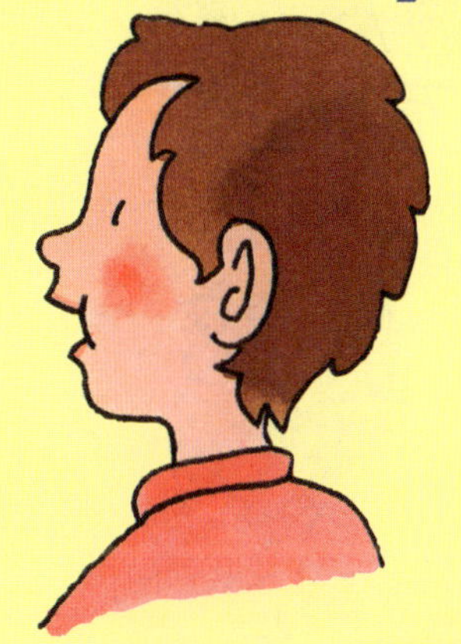

Parents: Read the words on page 78 to your child. He or she should know how to recite the days of the week in order, but not necessarily how to read the words.

Skill: Naming days of the week in order

Answers on page 126.

Calendar Fun

A calendar is a list of all the days, weeks, and months of the year. You will find dates on a calendar. Willy's calendar has some days without numbers! Write the missing numbers.

June				
Sunday	**Monday**	**Tuesday**	**Wednesday**	**Thursday**
	1	2	3	
	8	9	10	
14 Flag Day		16		18
21 Father's Day	22		24	Willy's birthday
28		30		

Father's Day is on June _____ .

Flag Day is on June _____ .

Willy's birthday is on June _____ .

Willy will go camping on June _____ .

Parents: Teach this version of a traditional rhyme to help your child remember how many days are in each month:

Thirty days hath September,
April, June, and November.
All the rest have 31,
But February in 28 is done.

Skill: Reading a calendar

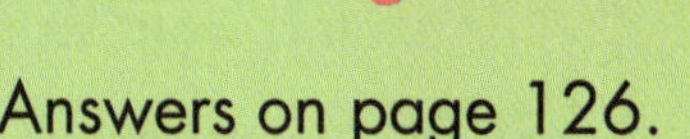
Answers on page 126.

Around the Year

A year has 4 seasons. Can you name the seasons in order? Use the pictures to help you.

spring

summer

fall

winter

Draw yourself during your favorite season. What season is it?

Parents: You may want to tell your child that another word for *fall* is *autumn*.

Skill: Naming seasons in order

Answers will vary.

First to the Finish Line

The animals are having a race. Which animal is crossing the finish line first? Second? Third? Fourth? Fifth? Draw a line to match each winner with their prize.

Skill: Recognizing ordinal numbers first through fifth

Answers on page 126.

Share a Snack

A half is 1 of 2 pieces that are the same size.

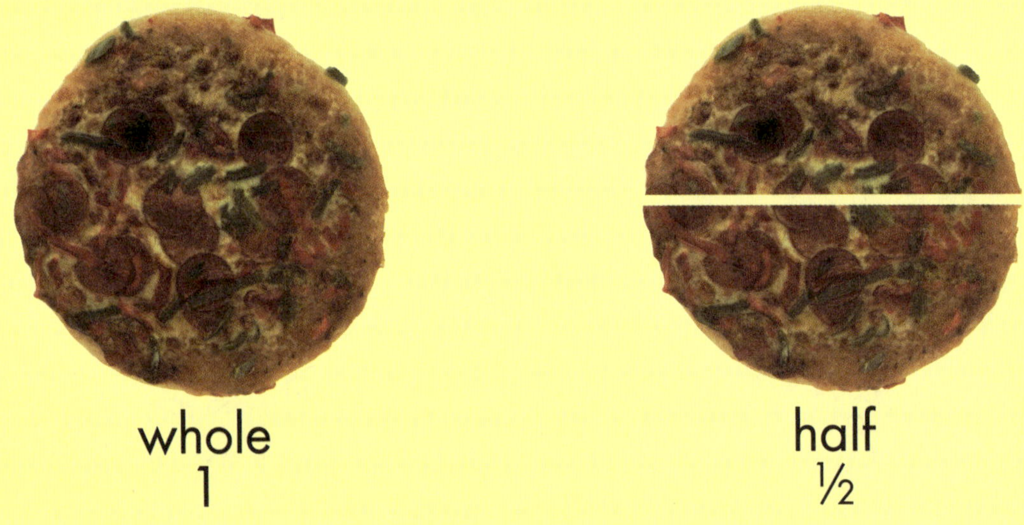

whole
1

half
½

Share with a friend. Draw lines to cut each snack in half.

Skill: Dividing whole objects into halves

Answers on page 126.

Fun with Food

Circle the picture that shows ½ of each food.

Parents: Point out real-life examples of fractions. For example, cut a piece of bread in half, saying, "I cut the whole slice of bread in half. Now I have two equal pieces."

Skill: Understanding whole and half

Answers on page 126.

Pick a Pet

Ask 5 people to pick a favorite pet. Pick your favorite pet, too. Put a mark like this / next to the pet's name each time someone picks it.

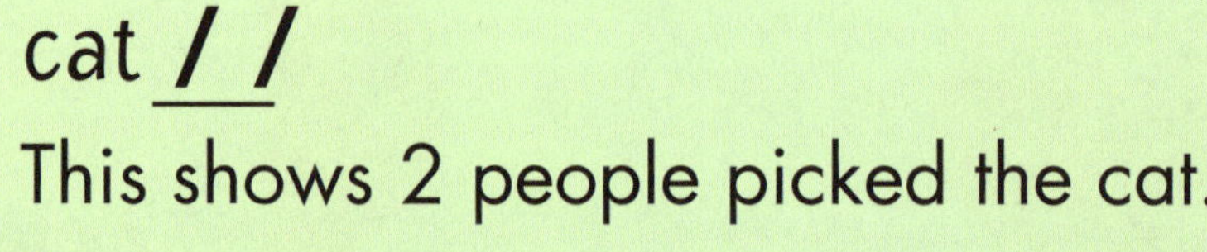

cat __/ /__

This shows 2 people picked the cat.

dog ____

fish ____

cat ____

rabbit ____

bird ____

Skill: Collecting data

Answers will vary.

Picture the Pets

Fill in the number of squares on the graph next to each animal's picture to show how many people picked that animal.

cat
2 people picked the cat. 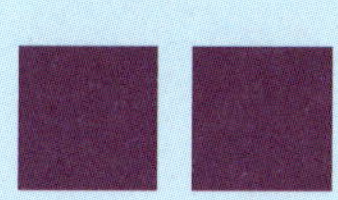

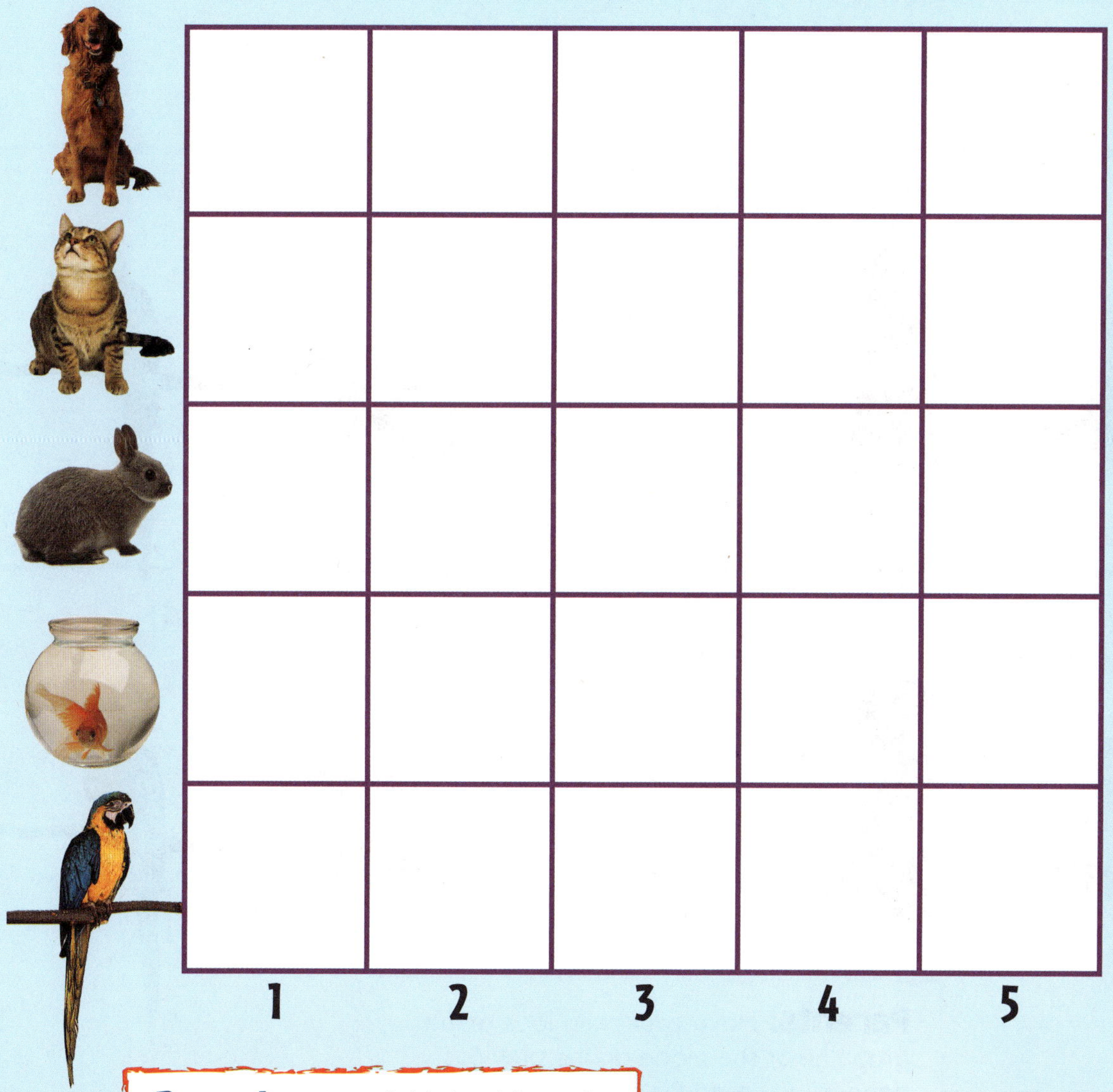

1	2	3	4	5

Parents: Your child should use the information collected on the previous page to make the graph.

Skill: Creating a pictograph

Answers will vary.

Read the Pictures

Look at the pictures you drew on the graph on page 87. Use them to answer these questions by writing the numbers.

How many people picked the cat? _____

How many people picked the fish? _____

How many people picked the dog? _____

How many people picked the rabbit? _____

How many people picked the bird? _____

What pet did most people pick? Circle it.

What pet did the fewest people pick? Circle it.

Parents: Have your child look at the graph he or she made on the previous page as you read the questions above.

Skill: Using a graph to answer questions

Answers will vary.

Count to 100!

You can count to 100! Touch each number as you say it.

1	2	3	4	5	6	7	8	9	10
11	12	13	14	15	16	17	18	19	20
21	22	23	24	25	26	27	28	29	30
31	32	33	34	35	36	37	38	39	40
41	42	43	44	45	46	47	48	49	50
51	52	53	54	55	56	57	58	59	60
61	62	63	64	65	66	67	68	69	70
71	72	73	74	75	76	77	78	79	80
81	82	83	84	85	86	87	88	89	90
91	92	93	94	95	96	97	98	99	100

Parents: Your child should know how to count from 1 to 100 accurately, even if he or she does not recognize the numerals themselves. If your child does recognize large numbers, say a number and have him or her locate it on the chart. You might want your child to circle the number as well.

Skill: Rote counting by 1s to 100

Count by 10s

You can count by 10s! Just read the numbers on the blue squares from top to bottom. Then trace the numbers with your pencil.

1	2	3	4	5	6	7	8	9	10
11	12	13	14	15	16	17	18	19	20
21	22	23	24	25	26	27	28	29	30
31	32	33	34	35	36	37	38	39	40
41	42	43	44	45	46	47	48	49	50
51	52	53	54	55	56	57	58	59	60
61	62	63	64	65	66	67	68	69	70
71	72	73	74	75	76	77	78	79	80
81	82	83	84	85	86	87	88	89	90
91	92	93	94	95	96	97	98	99	100

Parents: Have your child point to and say the numbers in the blue boxes as he or she counts by 10s.

Skill: Rote counting by 10s to 100

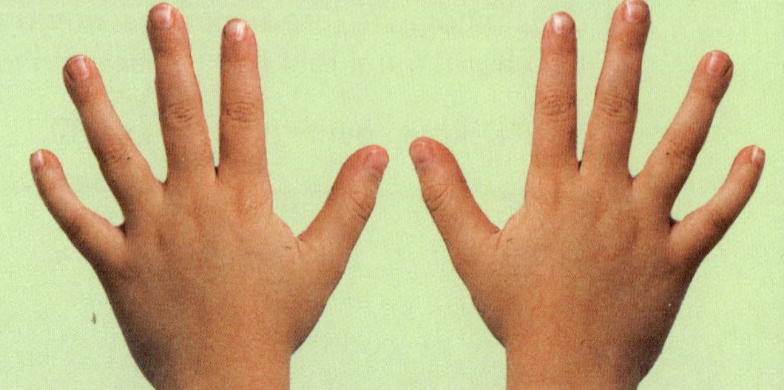

Count by 5s

You can count by 5s! Just read the numbers across in the orange columns. Then color the squares as you count by 5s again.

1	2	3	4	5	6	7	8	9	10
11	12	13	14	15	16	17	18	19	20
21	22	23	24	25	26	27	28	29	30
31	32	33	34	35	36	37	38	39	40
41	42	43	44	45	46	47	48	49	50
51	52	53	54	55	56	57	58	59	60
61	62	63	64	65	66	67	68	69	70
71	72	73	74	75	76	77	78	79	80
81	82	83	84	85	86	87	88	89	90
91	92	93	94	95	96	97	98	99	100

Parents: Have your child point to and say the numbers in the orange columns as he or she counts by 5s.

Skill: Rote counting by 5s to 100

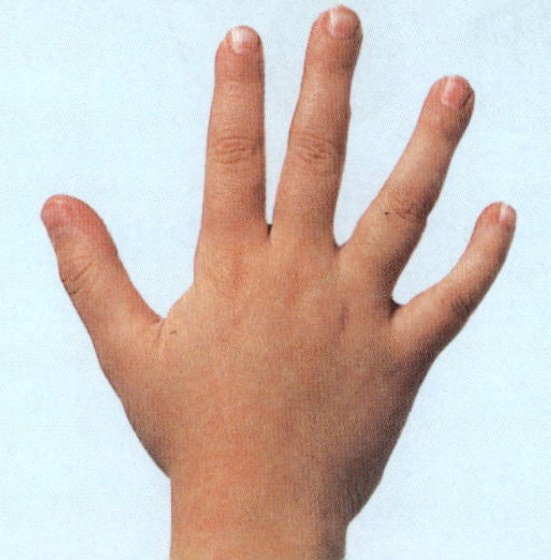

Counting Pennies

A penny and a cent are different names for the same coin.

1 cent
1¢

2 cents
2¢

3 cents
3¢

Count the sets of pennies. Draw lines to show what you can buy.

3¢

9¢

7¢

6¢

Skill: Understanding the value of a penny

Answers on page 126.

Counting Nickels

1 nickel is the same amount as 5 pennies.

5 cents
5¢

5 cents
5¢

Parents: You may want to have your child use the Counting by Fives chart on page 91 to complete this activity. Also, use real coins to help your child practice counting coins. First have him or her count the nickels by 5s, then continue counting by 1s to add the pennies and reach the total.

Skill: Understanding the value of a nickel

To find out how much money you have, count nickels by 5s.

5¢ 10¢ 15¢ 20¢ 25¢

5 nickels are the same amount of money as 25¢.

Circle the amount that shows how many cents each child has.

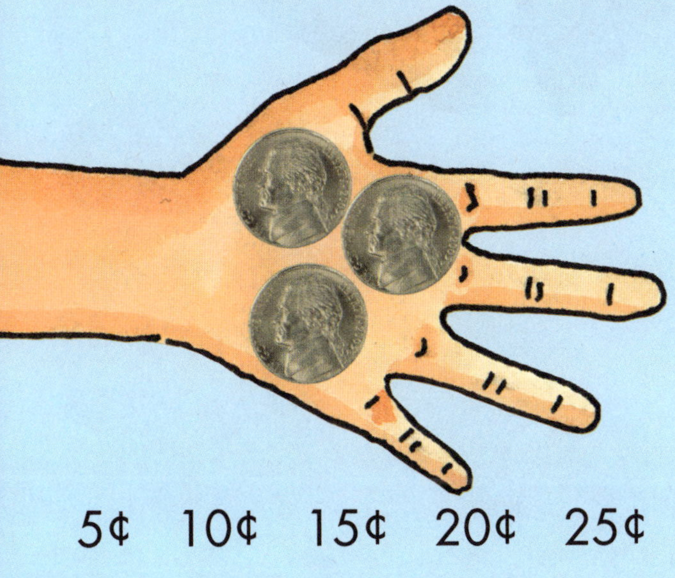

5¢ 10¢ 15¢ 20¢ 25¢

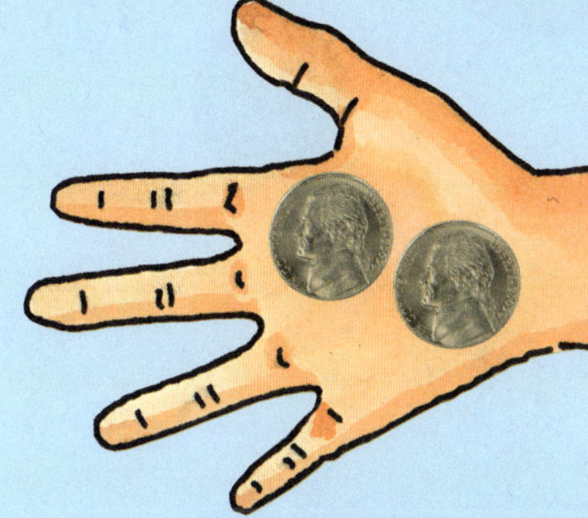

5¢ 10¢ 15¢ 20¢ 25¢

Answers on page 126.

Counting Dimes

1 dime is the same amount as 10 pennies.

10 cents
10¢

10 cents
10¢

Parents: You may want to have your child use the Counting by Tens chart on page 90.

Skill: Understanding the value of a dime

To find out how much money you have, count the dimes by 10s.

10¢

20¢

30¢

40¢

50¢

5 dimes are the same amount of money as 50¢.

Count the dimes by 10s. Write the amount. Draw lines between the money and the matching price tag.

Answers on page 126.

Counting Quarters

1 quarter is the same amount as 25 pennies.

25 cents
25¢

25 cents
25¢

You have 1 quarter. Circle what you can buy.

25¢

35¢

You have 1 quarter. Circle what you can buy.

50¢

25¢

You have 1 quarter. Circle what you can buy.

39¢

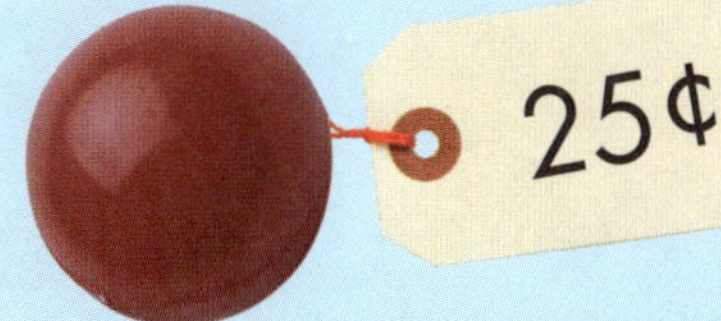

25¢

Parents: Look through an assortment of quarters with your child. Be sure your child understands that despite the different images on the back of each coin, each quarter is worth the same amount.

Skill: Understanding the value of a quarter

Answers on page 127.

Save Your Money!

The front of each coin looks different than the back.

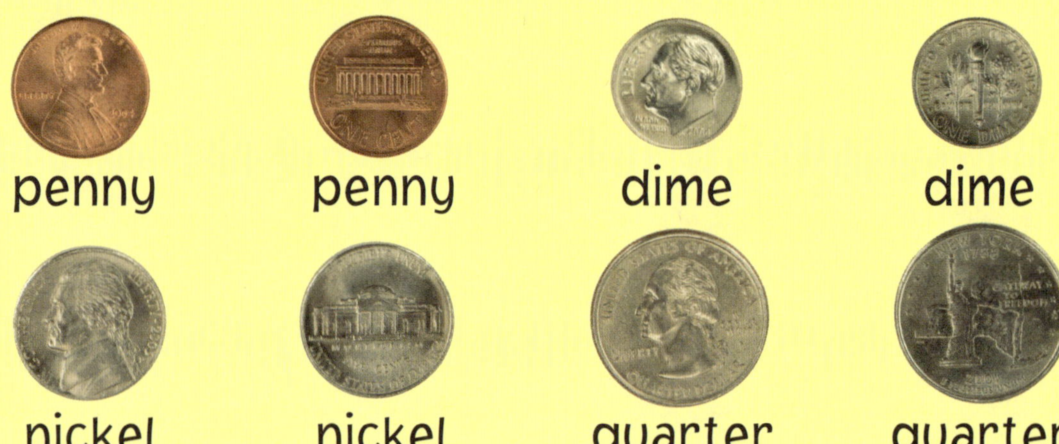

Draw lines to show into which bank each coin should go.

Parents: Help your child understand that the front and back of each coin are shown on this page. Look at real pennies and nickels together. Discuss how they might differ from the images shown here, but the size, shape, and color of each coin are still the same.

Skill: Recognizing coins

Answers on page 127.

Guess How Many

Guess how many stars are on the page. This is called an <u>estimate.</u> Now count and write the number of stars.

Guess: ________

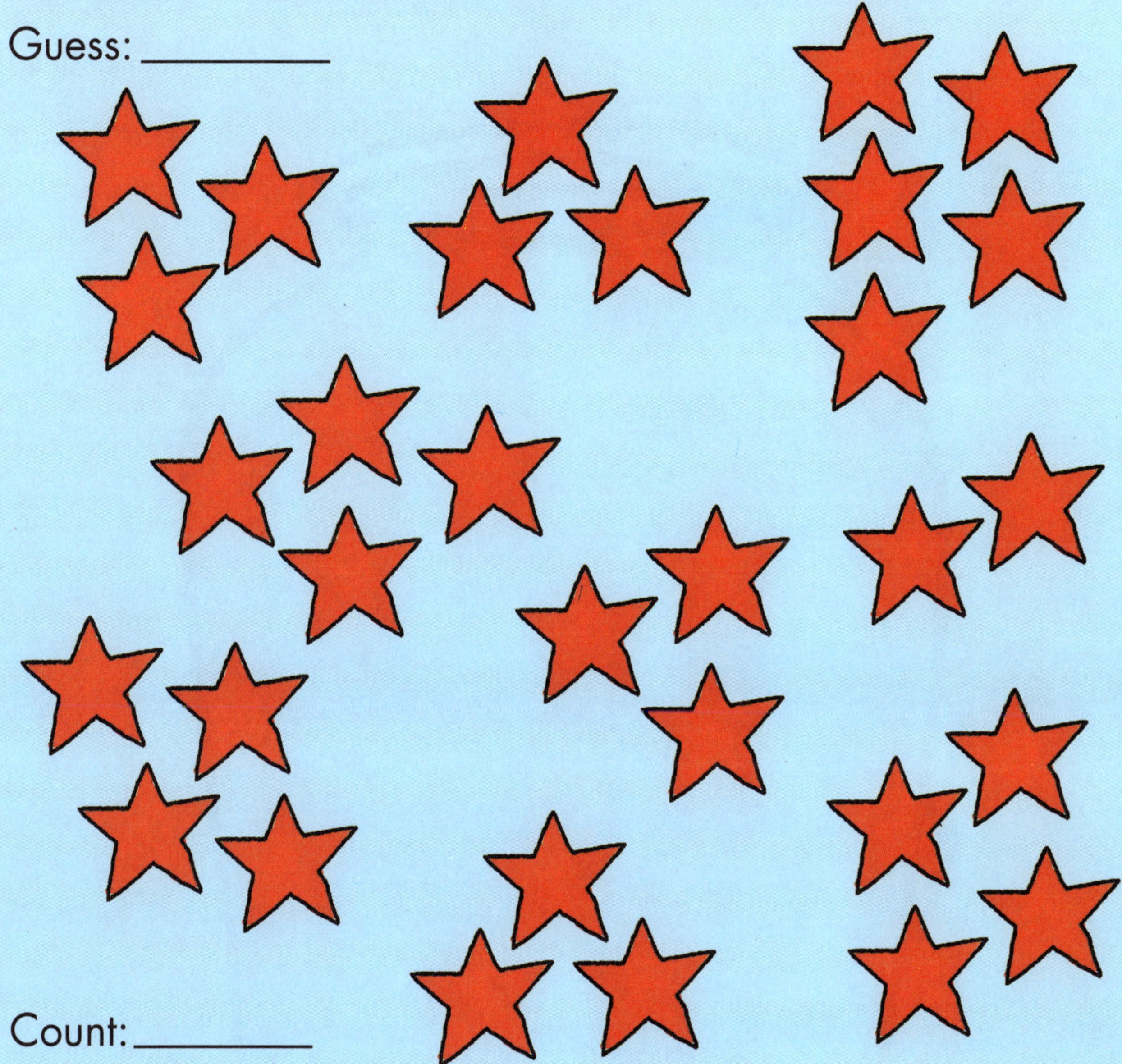

Count: ________

Parents: Remind your child to look quickly to guess, not count. Use real objects to provide more practice with estimating, then count to verify estimates.

Skill: Estimating larger numbers

Answers on page 127.

How Many Candies?

Draw some candy in the jar. Ask someone to <u>estimate</u> how many candies are inside.

Skill: Estimating numbers

Answers will vary.

Same or Different?

If things are the <u>same,</u> they look alike.

If things are <u>different,</u> they do not look alike.

same

different

Circle the word that tells about the pictures.

Parents: Ask your child to talk about these examples. Help him or her understand that things can be alike in some ways and different in others. For instance, even though the dinosaurs are the same because they are all dinosaurs, they are different because they are different shapes and different colors.

Skill: Understanding same and different

Answers on page 127.

Fair and Fun!

equal number of balloons

not equal number of balloons

Parents: Help your child understand that things can be equal in amount even if they are not exactly the same.

Skill: Understanding equal and unequal

Which sets are equal? Circle them.

Answers on page 127.

Two Sides the Same

Look at the shapes. Circle the shapes with two parts that look the same when they are folded or cut in two.

Parents: Things that are symmetrical can be cut into two parts that mirror one another. Give children practice with symmetry by making inkblot pictures. Fold a sheet of paper in half, then open it. Have your child put a small blob of paint on one side, then fold the paper again and press down. Unfold to see a symmetrical design.

Skill: Understanding symmetry

Answers on page 127.

More of the Same

On each object, draw a line to make two parts that look the same.

Skill: Drawing lines of symmetry

Answers on page 127.

Seaside Symmetry

Circle the objects with two parts that look the same.

Skill: Recognizing symmetry in nature

Answers on page 127.

Time to Tell

On a clock, the short hand points to the hour. The long hand points to the minute. Look at the clock. What number does the short hand point to? Write the hour.

_____ o'clock

_____ o'clock

_____ o'clock

_____ o'clock

_____ o'clock

_____ o'clock

Parents: Help your child understand that when the long hand points straight up to 12, it indicates *"on* the hour." The short hand is then pointing to the actual hour.

Skill: Telling time to the hour (analog clock)

Answers on page 127.

What Time Is It?

Draw the short hand on each clock. Then write the time.

Skill: Telling time to the hour (analog clock)

Answers will vary.

Look! No Hands!

Some clocks do not have hands. The first number tells the hour.

Skill: Telling time to the hour (digital clocks)

It is 4 o'clock

Circle the time when things happen.

7 o'clock 9 o'clock

5 o'clock 8 o'clock

6 o'clock 12 o'clock

2 o'clock 11 o'clock

Answers on page 127.

Putting Things Together

When 2 sets are put together, they are added to each other. This is called addition.

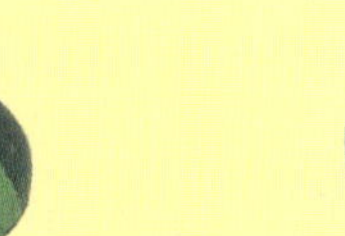

5 marbles

Draw more marbles to make a set of 5.

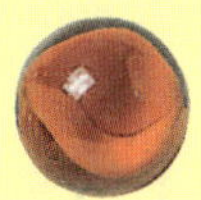

2 balloons

Draw more balloons to make a set of 2.

3 buttons

Draw more buttons to make a set of 3.

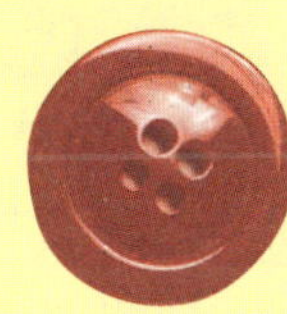

4 crayons

Draw more crayons to make a set of 4.

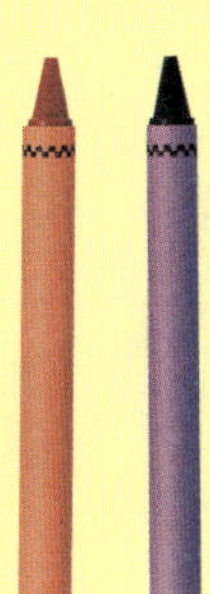

Parents: Have your child manipulate real objects around the home to create equivalent sets.

Skill: Creating equivalent sets

Answers on page 127.

Adding Animals

Count how many in all.

1 and 2 more is 3

2 and 2 more is ____

3 and 2 more is ____

4 and 1 more is ____

Parents: Encourage your child to count the pictures to find the totals. Provide practice with addition by making sets of objects for your child to add, such as 3 blocks and 2 blocks.

Skill: Understanding addition

Answers on page 127.

Signs for Adding

+	=
plus sign	equal sign
A plus sign means "and."	An equal sign means "is the same as."

2 and 2 is 4

2 + 2 = 4

Count to find out how many all together.

1 and 2 is ______

1 + 2 = ______

3 and 1 is ______

3 + 1 = ______

Skill: Recognizing the symbols + and =

Answers on page 127.

Ready, Add, Go!

Write the number of items in each set. Count to find out how many items in all.

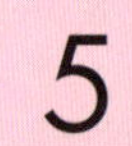

2 + 3 = 5

____ + ____ = ____

____ + ____ = ____

Skill: Solving addition facts with sums up to 5

____ + ____ = ____

Answers on page 127.

1, 2, 3, Add!

Write the number of items in each set. Count to find out how many items in all.

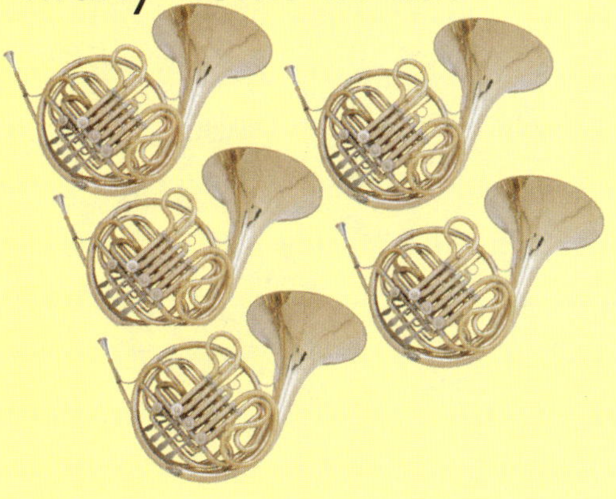

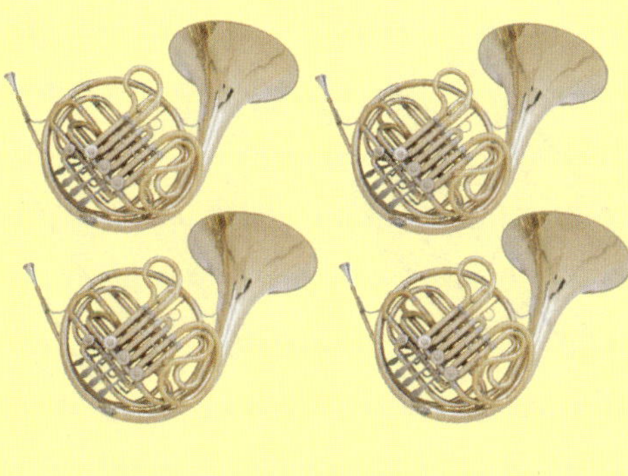

________ + ________ = ________

________ + ________ = ________

Skill: Solving addition facts with sums up to 10

________ + ________ = ________

Answers on page 127.

Add Some More

Look at the pictures. Write the number of items in each set. Tell how many items in all.

set 1 set 2

______ + ______ = ______

set 1 set 2

______ + ______ = ______

Draw and write your own number story here.

set 1 set 2

______ + ______ = ______

set 1 set 2

_______ + _______ = _______

set 1 set 2

_______ + _______ = _______

Draw and write another number story here.

set 1 set 2

_______ + _______ = _______

Skill: Reviewing addition up to 10

Answers on page 128.

It's Nothing

The number 0 is zero. Zero means "nothing."

Count the kittens in each basket. Write the number on the line below.

_______ _______ _______

Count the birds on each branch. Write the number on the line below.

_______ _______ _______

Count the fish in each bowl. Write the number on the line below.

Skill: Understanding the concept of zero

_______ _______ _______

Answers on page 128.

Take Some Away

An X has been put on something to take it away. This is called <u>subtraction.</u> Count how many are left.

3 take away 1 is __2__

5 take away 2 is ______

4 take away 2 is ______

5 take away 5 is ______

Parents: Have your child use objects to practice the concept of subtraction. Display 5 objects, and have your child count them. Then take 2 objects away and ask, "How many are left?"

Skill: Understanding the concept of taking away to subtract

Answers on page 128.

Signs for Subtracting

minus sign –

A minus sign means "take away."

4 take away 2 is 2

4 – 2 = 2

Put an X on 1 bird to take it away (subtract it). Now count to find out how many birds are left.

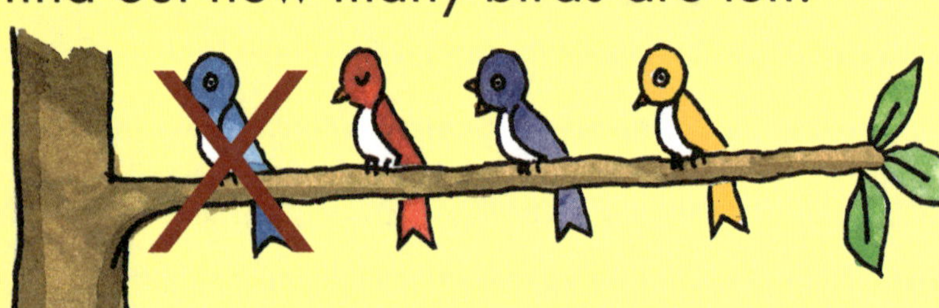

4 take away 1 is ____

4 – 1 = ____

5 take away 3 is ____

5 – 3 = ____

5 take away 2 is ____

5 – 2 = ____

Skill: Recognizing the symbol –

Answers on page 128.

What Is Left?

Put an X on the candies to take the right number away. Count how many candies are left.

6 – 2 = 4

8 – 1 = ____

4 – 2 = ____

5 – 5 = ____

7 – 3 = ____

Skill: Solving subtraction facts to 10

Answers on page 128.

Bye-Bye, Birdie

Count and write how many animals are in each set. Put an X on the animals you'd like to take away. Write that number. Count and write how many are left.

5 take away 2 is 3

$5 - 2 = 3$

___ – ___ = ___

___ – ___ = ___

Skill: Reviewing subtraction

Answers on page 128.

Another Way to Add

Count the top set of bugs. Count the set under it. Count both sets together. Write the number in the box.

4
+ 2
6

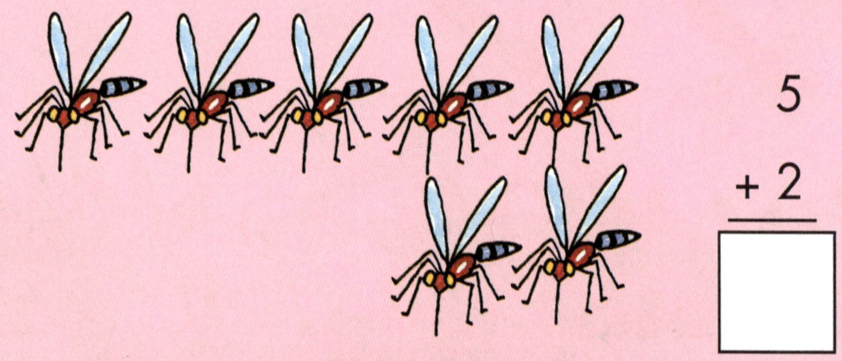

5
+ 2

2
+ 4

3
+ 1

Parents: Explain to your child that the line under the second number means the same as the equal symbol.

Skill: Understanding vertical addition

Answers on page 128.

Another Way to Subtract

Count the top set of each group. Count the set under it. Take away that number from the top set. Write that number in the box.

$$\begin{array}{r} 4 \\ -\ 2 \\ \hline 2 \end{array}$$

$$\begin{array}{r} 5 \\ -\ 2 \\ \hline \square \end{array}$$

$$\begin{array}{r} 4 \\ -\ 2 \\ \hline \square \end{array}$$

$$\begin{array}{r} 3 \\ -\ 1 \\ \hline \square \end{array}$$

Skill: Understanding vertical subtraction

Answers on page 128.

Answer Pages

Number Fun

Count how many steps the bird took. Trace the numbers on the bottom of the page. Then write them all by yourself!

1 2 3 4 5 6 7 8 9 10

page 10 page 11

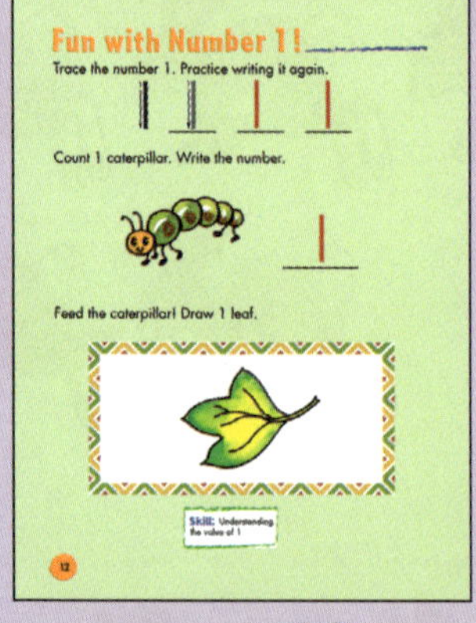
Fun with Number 1!

Trace the number 1. Practice writing it again.

Count 1 caterpillar. Write the number.

Feed the caterpillar! Draw 1 leaf.

page 12

Who's for 2?

Trace the number 2. Practice writing it again.

Count 2 anteaters. Write the number.

Feed the anteaters! Draw 2 ants.

page 13

Come and See the Number 3!

Trace the number 3. Practice writing it again.

Count 3 spiders. Write the number.

Feed the spiders! Draw 3 flies.

page 14

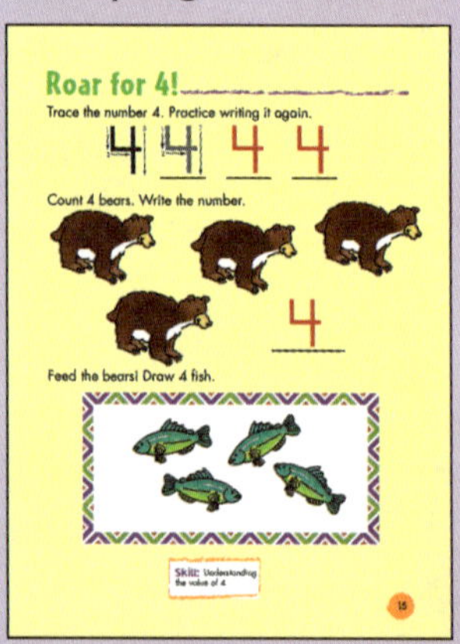
Roar for 4!

Trace the number 4. Practice writing it again.

Count 4 bears. Write the number.

Feed the bears! Draw 4 fish.

page 15

Dive for 5!

Trace the number 5. Practice writing it again.

Count 5 seagulls. Write the number.

Feed the seagulls! Draw 5 little fish.

page 16

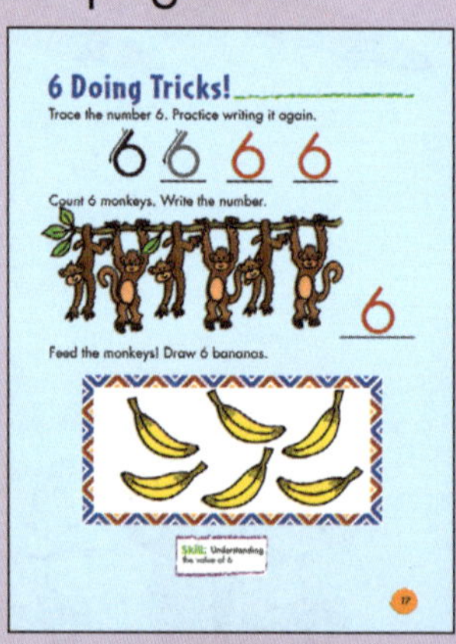
6 Doing Tricks!

Trace the number 6. Practice writing it again.

Count 6 monkeys. Write the number.

Feed the monkeys! Draw 6 bananas.

page 17

Hippety-Hop to 7!

Trace the number 7. Practice writing it again.

Count 7 rabbits. Write the number.

Feed the rabbits! Draw 7 carrots.

page 18

Number 8 Is Really Great!

Trace the number 8. Practice writing it again.

Count 8 bees. Write the number.

Feed the bees! Draw 8 flowers.

page 19

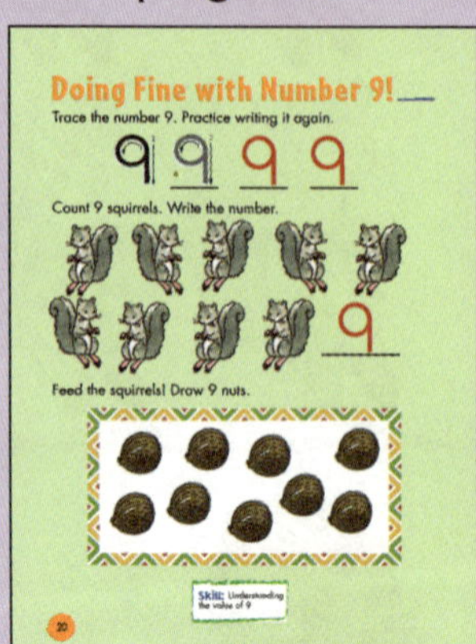
Doing Fine with Number 9!

Trace the number 9. Practice writing it again.

Count 9 squirrels. Write the number.

Feed the squirrels! Draw 9 nuts.

page 20

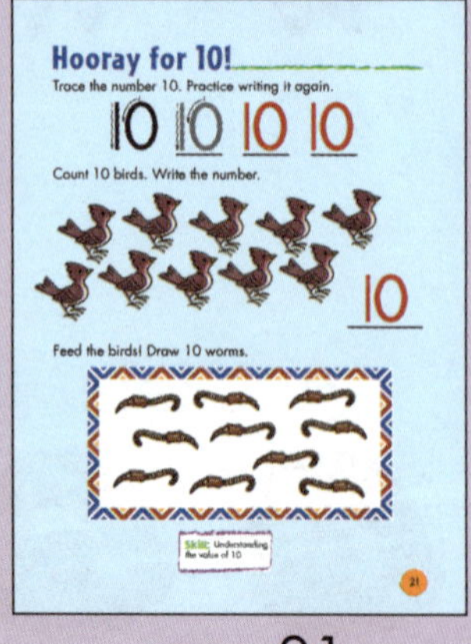
Hooray for 10!

Trace the number 10. Practice writing it again.

Count 10 birds. Write the number.

Feed the birds! Draw 10 worms.

page 21

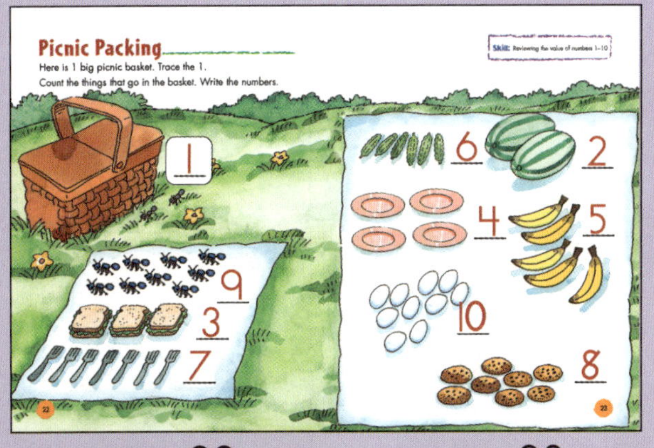

page 22 page 23

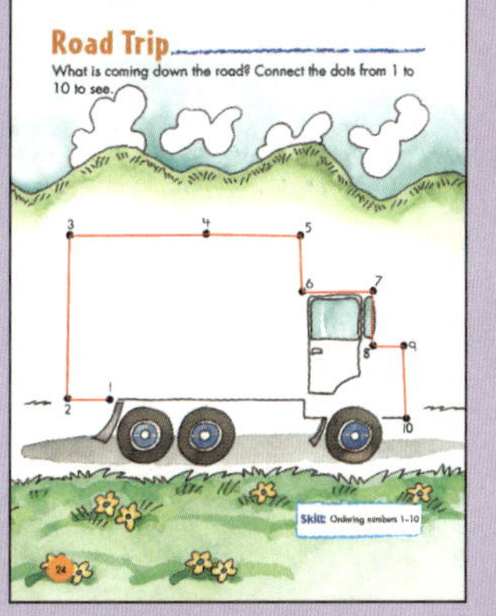

page 24

page 25

page 26

page 27

page 28

page 29

page 30

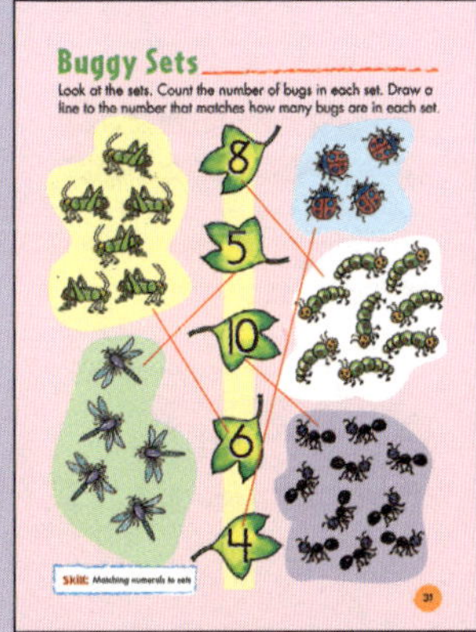

page 31

page 33

page 34

page 35

page 36

page 37

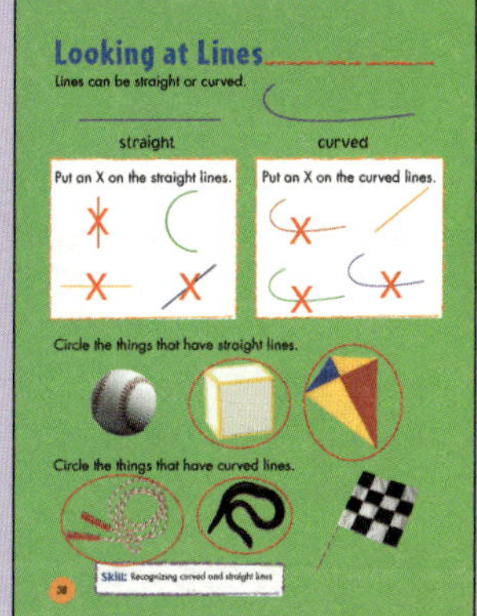

page 38

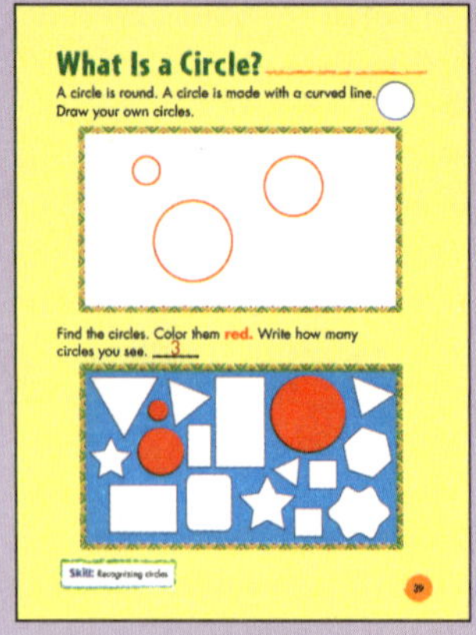
What Is a Circle?

A circle is round. A circle is made with a curved line. Draw your own circles.

Find the circles. Color them red. Write how many circles you see. 3

page 39

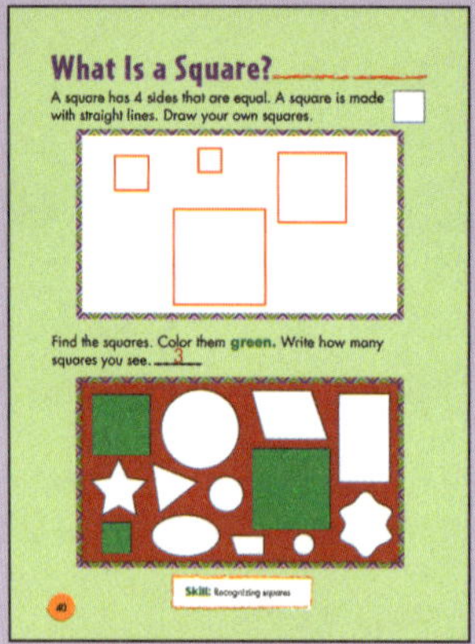
What Is a Square?

A square has 4 sides that are equal. A square is made with straight lines. Draw your own squares.

Find the squares. Color them green. Write how many squares you see. 3

page 40

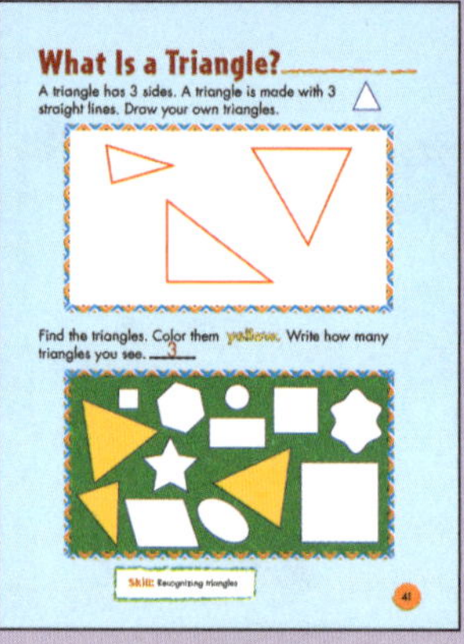
What Is a Triangle?

A triangle has 3 sides. A triangle is made with 3 straight lines. Draw your own triangles.

Find the triangles. Color them yellow. Write how many triangles you see. 3

page 41

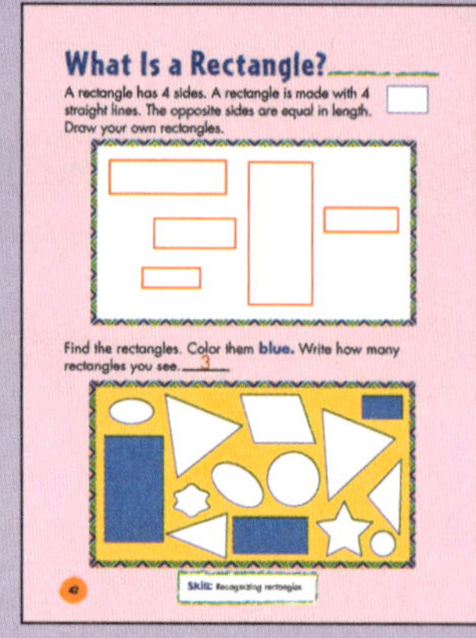
What Is a Rectangle?

A rectangle has 4 sides. A rectangle is made with 4 straight lines. The opposite sides are equal in length. Draw your own rectangles.

Find the rectangles. Color them blue. Write how many rectangles you see. 3

page 42

Shape Hunt

Shapes are everywhere! Just look around.

Put an X on the things that are circles.

Put an X on the things that are squares.

Put an X on the things that are triangles.

Put an X on the things that are rectangles.

page 43

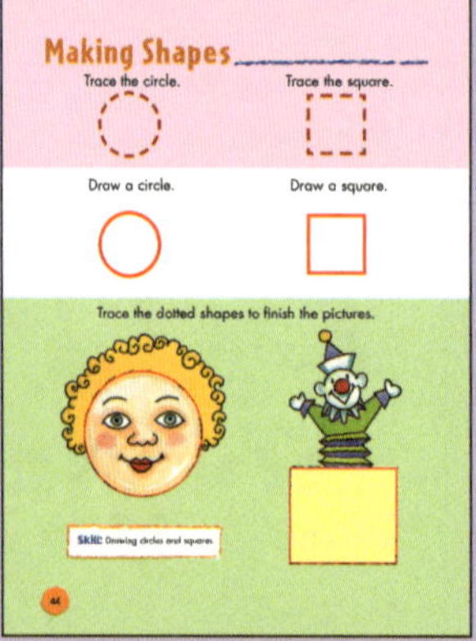
Making Shapes

Trace the circle. Trace the square.

Draw a circle. Draw a square.

Trace the dotted shapes to finish the pictures.

page 44

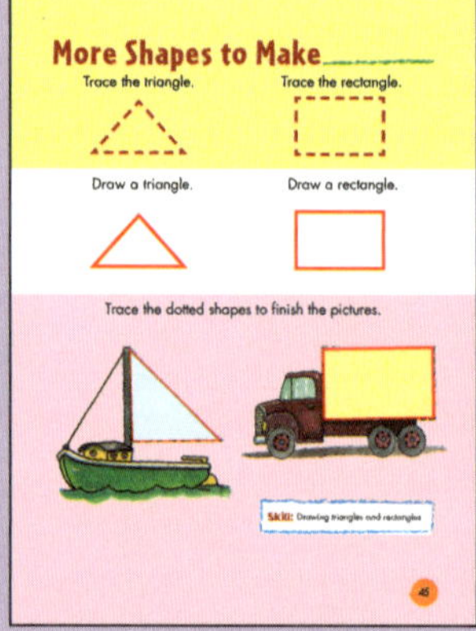
More Shapes to Make

Trace the triangle. Trace the rectangle.

Draw a triangle. Draw a rectangle.

Trace the dotted shapes to finish the pictures.

page 45

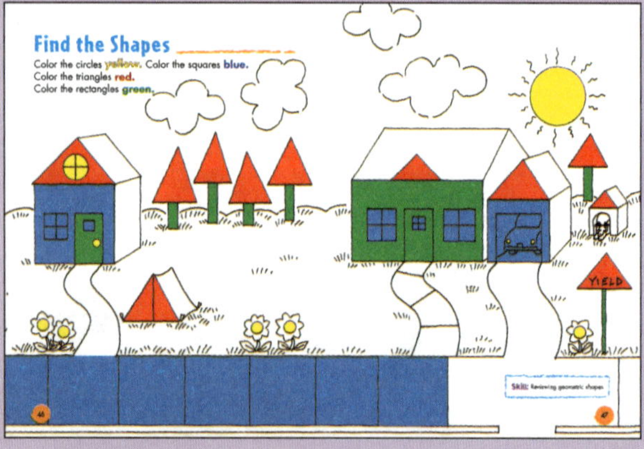
Find the Shapes

Color the circles yellow. Color the squares blue. Color the triangles red. Color the rectangles green.

page 46 page 47

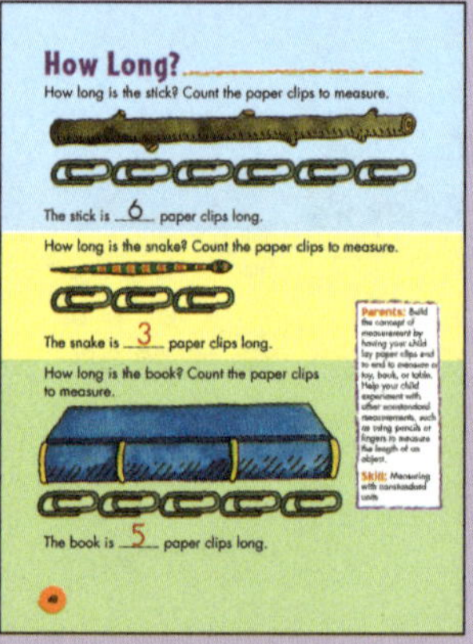
How Long?

How long is the stick? Count the paper clips to measure.

The stick is 6 paper clips long.

How long is the snake? Count the paper clips to measure.

The snake is 3 paper clips long.

How long is the book? Count the paper clips to measure.

The book is 5 paper clips long.

page 48

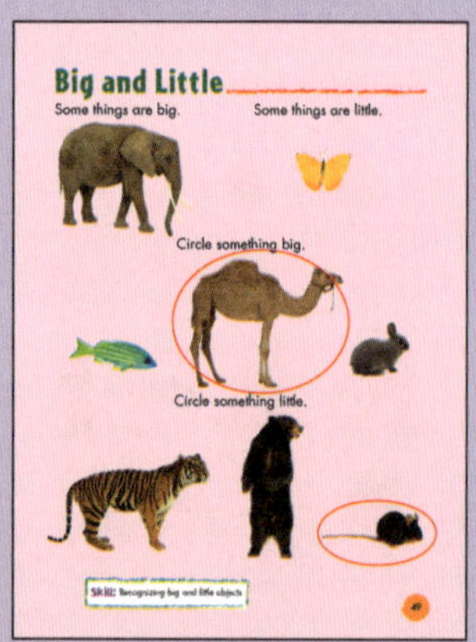
Big and Little

Some things are big. Some things are little.

Circle something big.

Circle something little.

page 49

Long and Short

Some animals are long. Some animals are short.

Circle the word that describes the animal's tail.

long short long short long short long short

Draw a long tail on the horse. Draw a short tail on the rabbit.

page 50

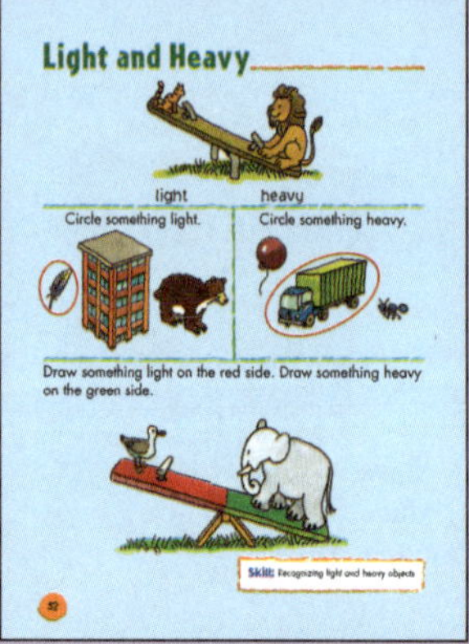
Light and Heavy

light heavy

Circle something light. Circle something heavy.

Draw something light on the red side. Draw something heavy on the green side.

page 52

Think About Size

Put an X on the tallest tree.

Put an X on the biggest dog.

Put an X on the littlest butterfly.

Put an X on the shortest crayon.

page 53

Full and Empty

full empty

Circle the things that are full. Put an X on the things that are empty.

page 54

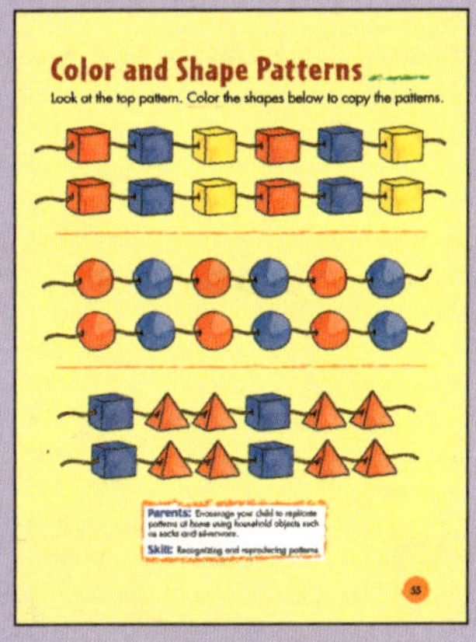
Color and Shape Patterns
Look at the top pattern. Color the shapes below to copy the patterns.

page 55

What Comes Next?
Look at the patterns. Draw what comes next.
Draw what comes next.
Draw what comes next.
Write what comes next.
1 2 3 1 2 3 1
2
Draw what comes next.
4 3 2 1 4 3 2 1

page 56 page 57

Before and After at the Zoo
The monkey had a banana before he ate it.
The banana was gone after the monkey ate it.
before after
Draw lines to match the words to the pictures.
before after before after

page 58

A Number Party
Can you count how many presents Marie received for her birthday? Trace the numbers. Now write the numbers on the lines.
1 1 2 2 3 3 4 4 5 5 6 6 7 7 8 8 9 9 10 10
11 11 12 12 13 13 14 14 15 15 16 16 17 17 18 18 19 19 20 20

page 60 page 61

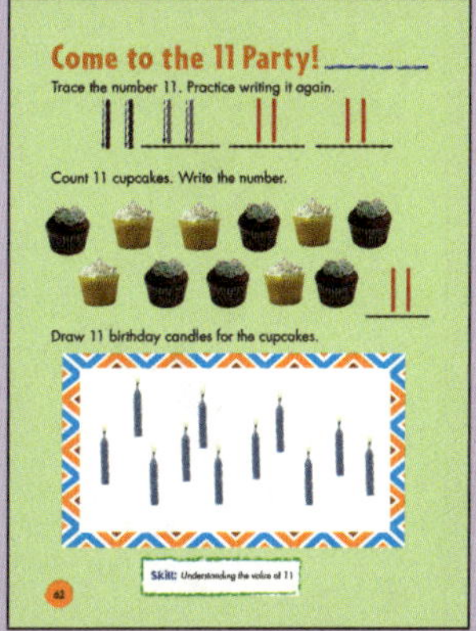
Come to the 11 Party!
Trace the number 11. Practice writing it again.
Count 11 cupcakes. Write the number.
11
Draw 11 birthday candles for the cupcakes.

page 62

12 Party Plates
Trace the number 12. Practice writing it again.
Count 12 party plates. Write the number.
12
Draw 12 scoops of ice cream for the plates.

page 63

13 Candles
Trace the number 13. Practice writing it again.
Count 13 candles. Write the number.
13
Draw 13 pieces of cake for the candles.

page 64

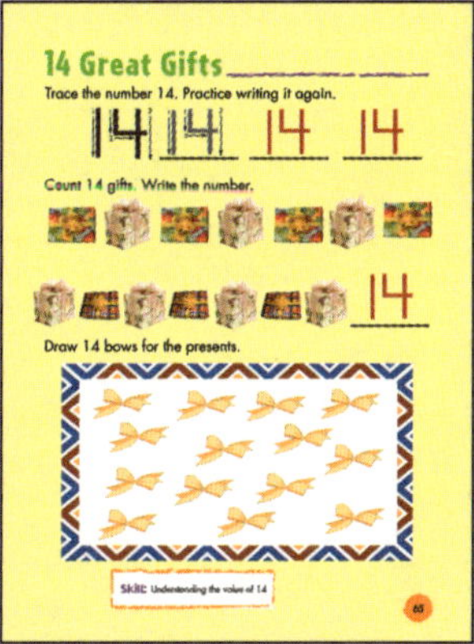
14 Great Gifts
Trace the number 14. Practice writing it again.
Count 14 gifts. Write the number.
14
Draw 14 bows for the presents.

page 65

15 Pretzels
Trace the number 15. Practice writing it again.
Count 15 pretzels. Write the number.
15
Draw 15 blobs of mustard for the pretzels.

page 66

16 Kids
Trace the number 16. Practice writing it again.
Count 16 kids. Write the number.
16
Draw 16 balloons for the kids.

page 67

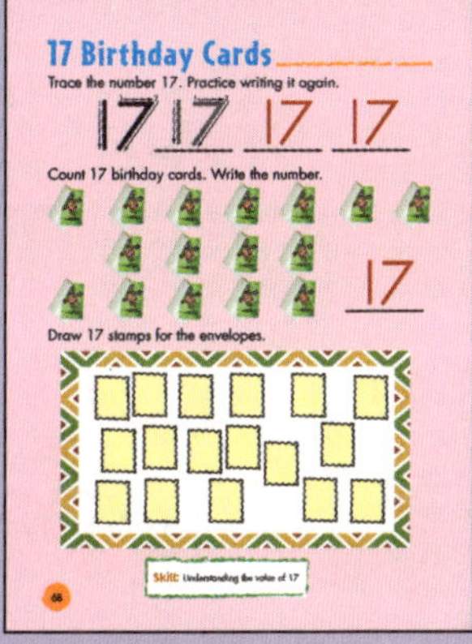
17 Birthday Cards
Trace the number 17. Practice writing it again.
Count 17 birthday cards. Write the number.
17
Draw 17 stamps for the envelopes.

page 68

18 Balloons
Trace the number 18. Practice writing it again.
Count 18 balloons. Write the number.
18
Draw 18 curvy pieces of string for the balloons.

page 69

19 Party Hats
Trace the number 19. Practice writing it again.
Count 19 hats. Write the number.
19
Draw 19 pom-poms for the hats.

page 70

20 Treats
Trace the number 20. Practice writing it again.
Count 20 lollipops. Write the number.
20
Draw 20 sticks for the lollipops.

page 71

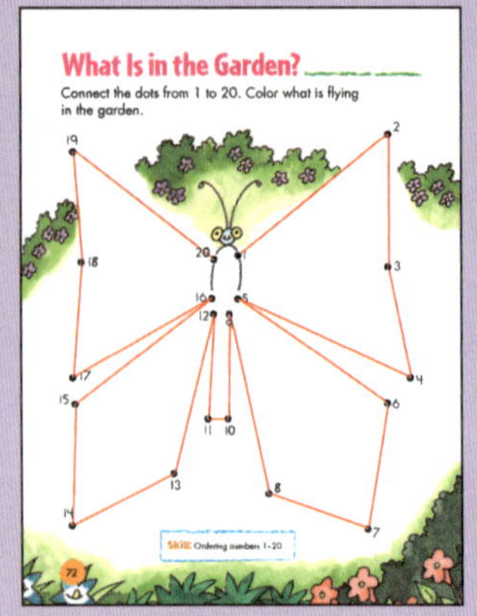
What Is in the Garden?
Connect the dots from 1 to 20. Color what is flying in the garden.

page 72

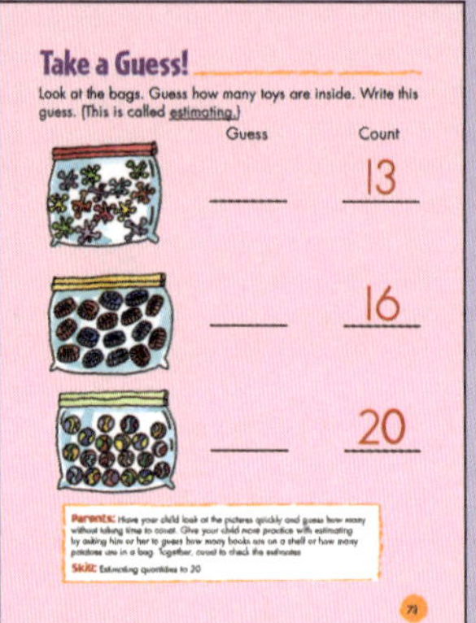
Take a Guess!
Look at the bags. Guess how many toys are inside. Write this guess. (This is called estimating.)

Guess	Count
	13
	16
	20

page 73

Numbers on Parade
Touch each little elephant in the parade above. Say the number out loud. Touch each big elephant in the parade below. Say the number out loud. Write the number on the line.

21 22 23 24 25 26 27 28 29 30 31

page 74 page 75

Who Is Hiding?
Who is hiding in the swamp? Connect the dots from 1 to 31 to find out. Then color the swamp creature.

page 76

Willy's Week
A week has 7 days. Say the days of the week in order. Use the pictures to help you read. What will Willy do each day of the week?

Sunday — Have a picnic.
Monday — Play ball.
Tuesday — Go swimming.
Wednesday — Play with toys.
Thursday — Go to the park.
Friday — Wash the dog.
Saturday — Go for a ride.

Circle the day that comes before Tuesday.
Saturday Monday

Circle the day that comes before Friday.
Thursday Sunday

Circle the day that comes after Saturday.
Sunday Tuesday

Circle the day that comes after Tuesday.
Friday Wednesday

page 78 page 79

Calendar Fun
A calendar is a list of all the days, weeks, and months of the year. You will find dates on a calendar. Willy's calendar has some days without numbers! Write the missing numbers.

June

Sunday	Monday	Tuesday	Wednesday	Thursday	Friday	Saturday
	1	2	3	4	5	6
7	8	9	10	11	12	13 camping
14 Flag Day	15	16	17	18	19	20
21 Father's Day	22	23	24	25 Willy's birthday	26	27
28	29	30				

Father's Day is on June 21.
Flag Day is on June 14.
Willy's birthday is on June 25.
Willy will go camping on June 13.

page 80 page 81

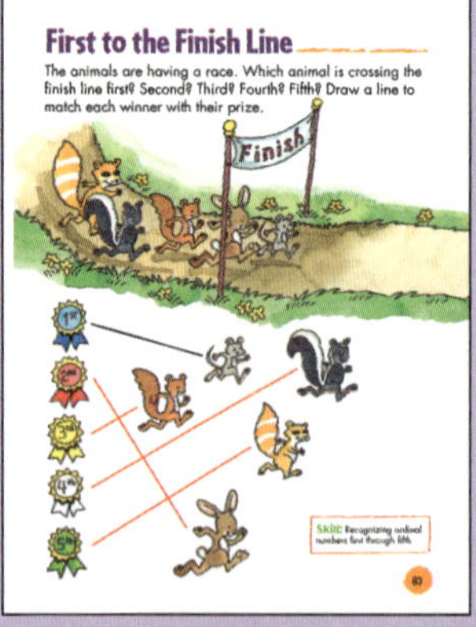
First to the Finish Line
The animals are having a race. Which animal is crossing the finish line first? Second? Third? Fourth? Fifth? Draw a line to match each winner with their prize.

page 83

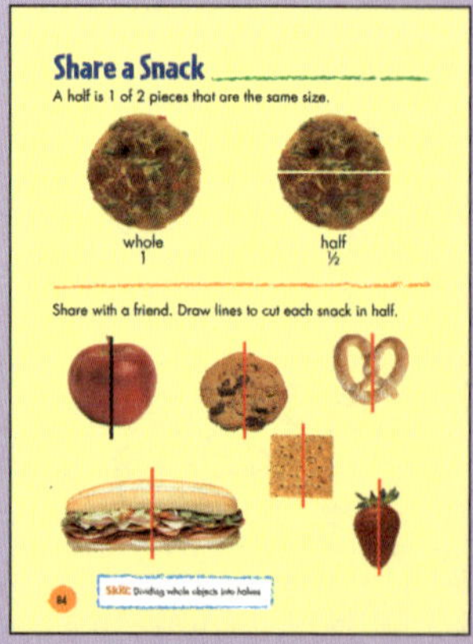
Share a Snack
A half is 1 of 2 pieces that are the same size.

whole 1 half ½

Share with a friend. Draw lines to cut each snack in half.

page 84

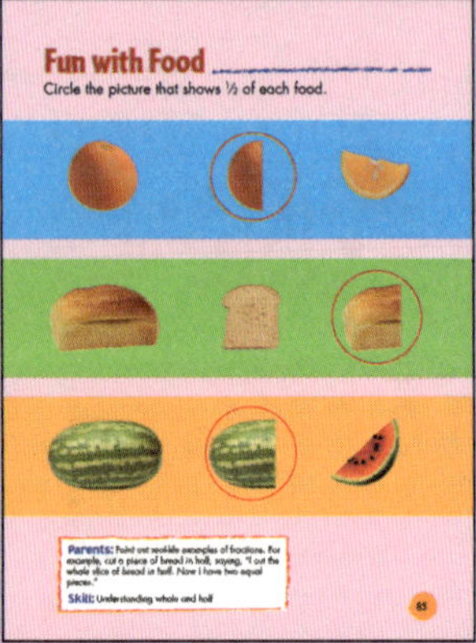
Fun with Food
Circle the picture that shows ½ of each food.

page 85

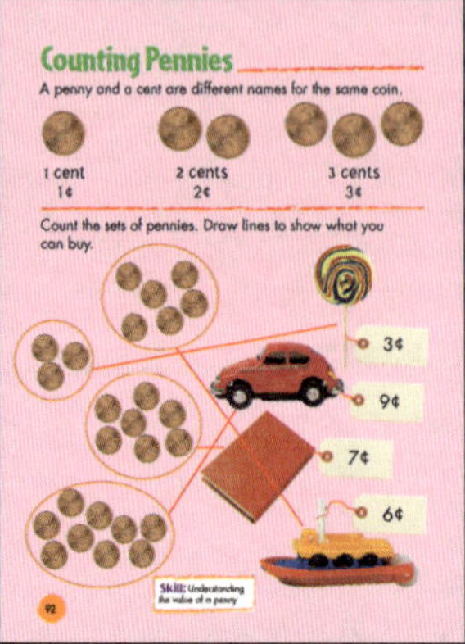
Counting Pennies
A penny and a cent are different names for the same coin.

1 cent 1¢ 2 cents 2¢ 3 cents 3¢

Count the sets of pennies. Draw lines to show what you can buy.

3¢ 9¢ 7¢ 6¢

page 92

Counting Nickels
1 nickel is the same amount as 5 pennies.

5 cents 5¢ 5 cents 5¢

To find out how much money you have, count nickels by 5s.

5¢ 10¢ 15¢ 20¢ 25¢

5 nickels are the same amount of money as 25¢.

Circle the amount that shows how many cents each child has.

5¢ 10¢ 15¢ 20¢ 25¢ 5¢ 10¢ 15¢ 20¢ 25¢

page 93

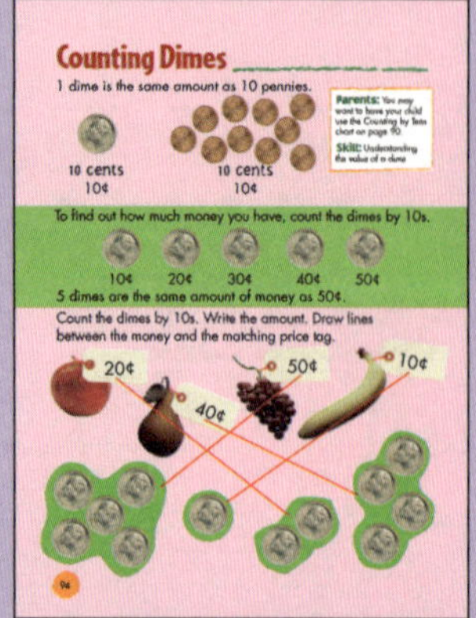
Counting Dimes
1 dime is the same amount as 10 pennies.

10 cents 10¢ 10 cents 10¢

To find out how much money you have, count the dimes by 10s.

10¢ 20¢ 30¢ 40¢ 50¢

5 dimes are the same amount of money as 50¢.

Count the dimes by 10s. Write the amount. Draw lines between the money and the matching price tag.

20¢ 40¢ 50¢ 10¢

page 94

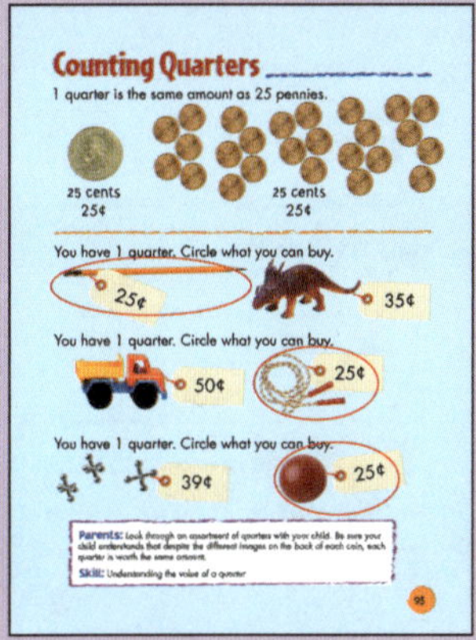

page 95

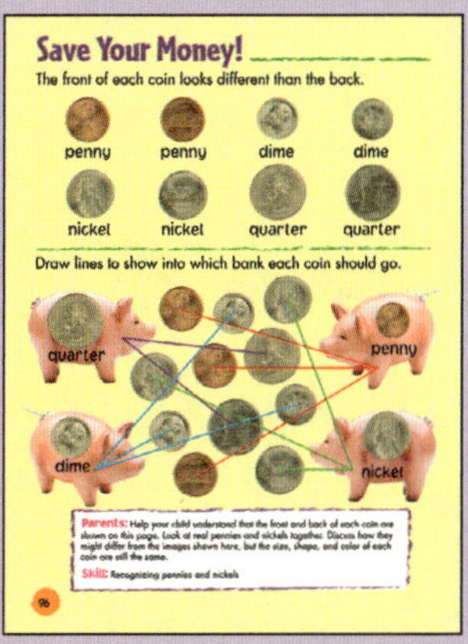

page 96

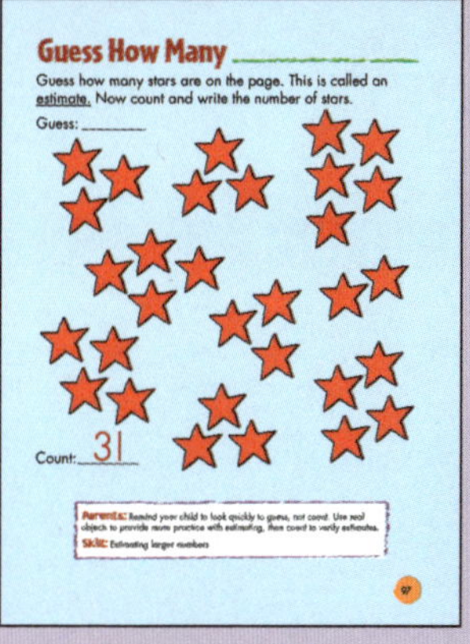

page 97

page 99

page 100

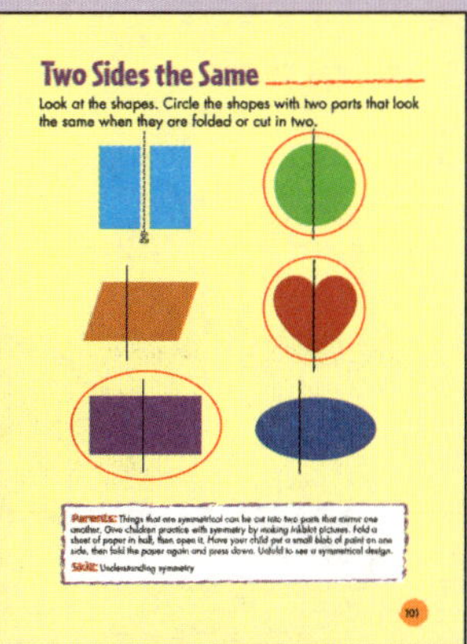

page 101

page 102

page 103

page 104

page 106

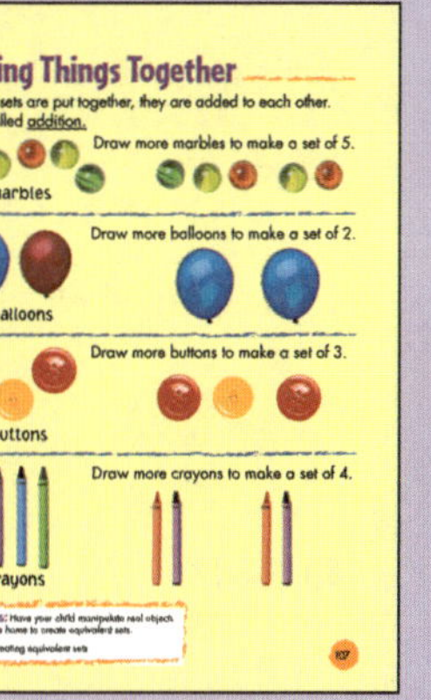

page 107

page 108

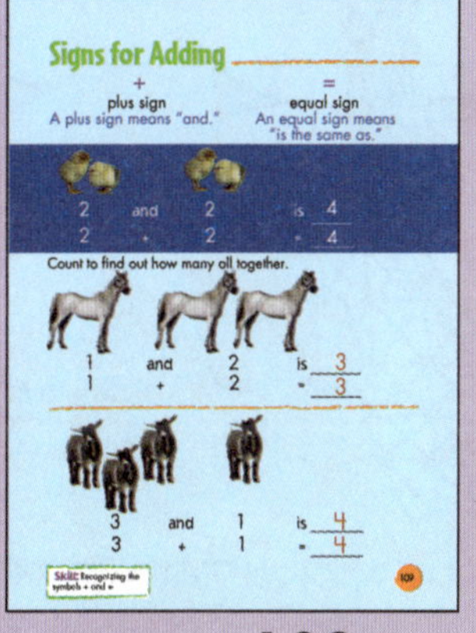

page 109

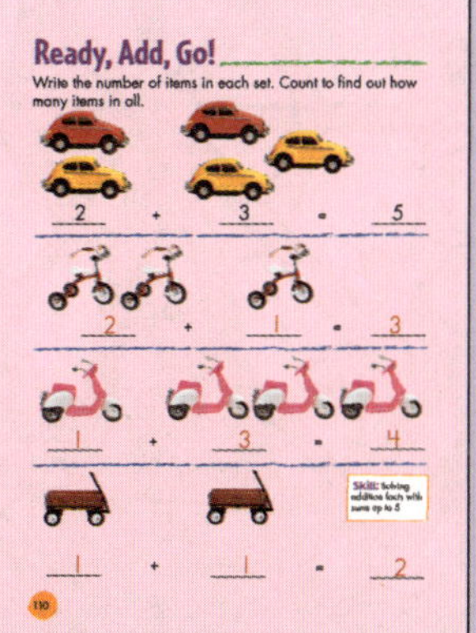

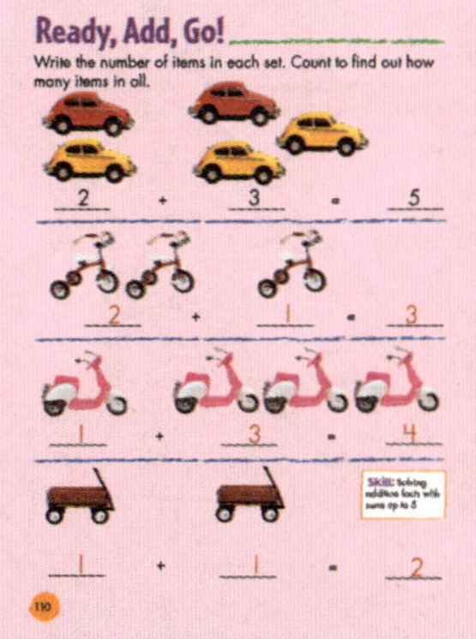

page 110

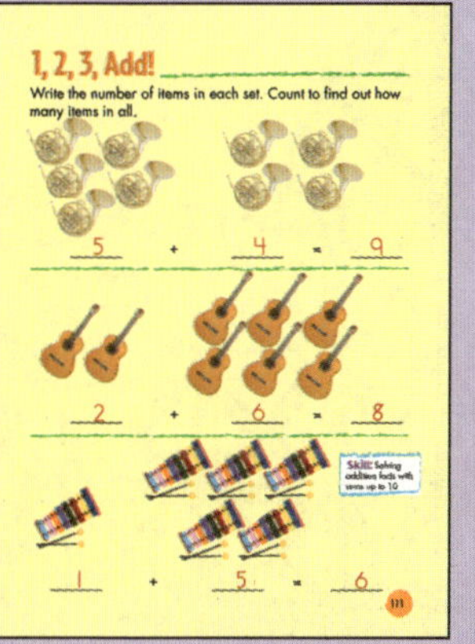

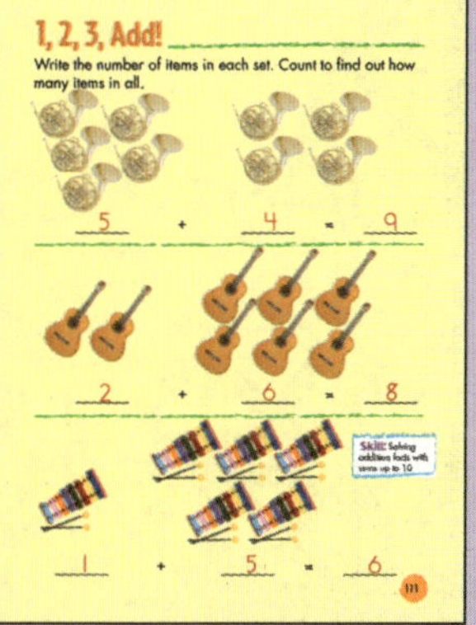

page 111

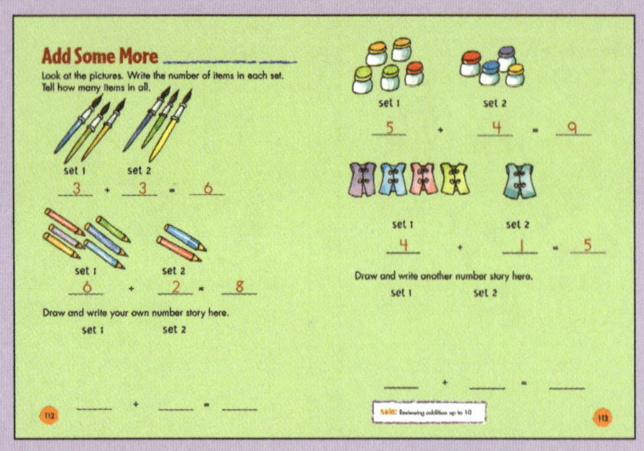
Add Some More

Look at the pictures. Write the number of items in each set. Tell how many items in all.

set 1 set 2
3 + 3 = 6

set 1 set 2
6 + 2 = 8

Draw and write your own number story here.

set 1 set 2

___ + ___ = ___

set 1 set 2
5 + 4 = 9

set 1 set 2
4 + 1 = 5

Draw and write another number story here.

set 1 set 2

___ + ___ = ___

Skill: Reviewing addition up to 10

page 112 page 113

It's Nothing

The number 0 is zero. Zero means "nothing."

2 4 0

Count the kittens in each basket. Write the number on the line below.

3 0 4

Count the birds on each branch. Write the number on the line below.

5 1 0

Count the fish in each bowl. Write the number on the line below.

0 6 4

Skill: Understanding the concept of zero

page 114

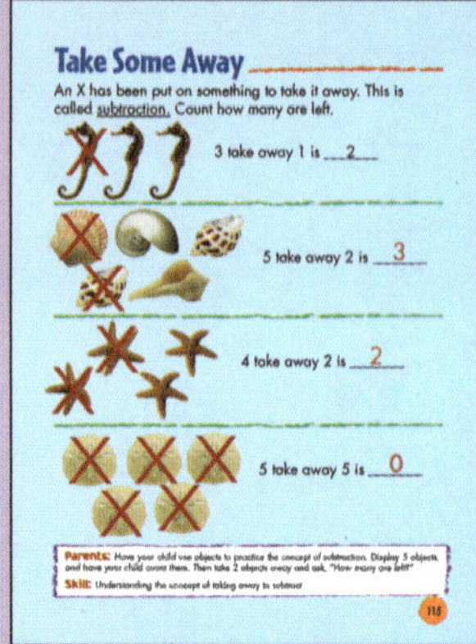
Take Some Away

An X has been put on something to take it away. This is called subtraction. Count how many are left.

3 take away 1 is 2

5 take away 2 is 3

4 take away 2 is 2

5 take away 5 is 0

Parents: Have your child use objects to practice the concept of subtraction. Display 5 objects, and have your child count them. Then take 2 objects away and ask, "How many are left?"

Skill: Understanding the concept of taking away to subtract

page 115

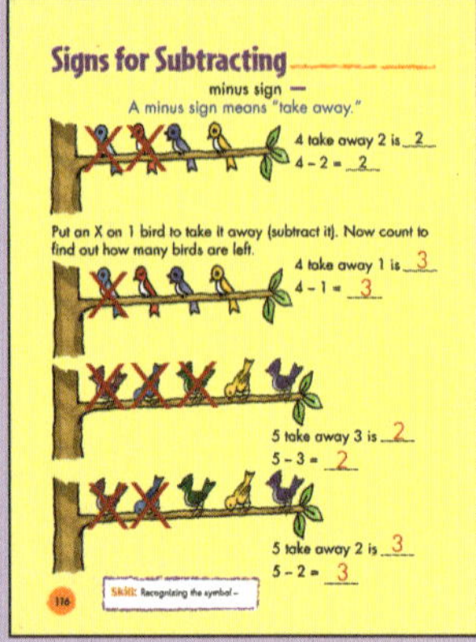
Signs for Subtracting

minus sign —

A minus sign means "take away."

4 take away 2 is 2
4 − 2 = 2

Put an X on 1 bird to take it away (subtract it). Now count to find out how many birds are left.

4 take away 1 is 3
4 − 1 = 3

5 take away 3 is 2
5 − 3 = 2

5 take away 2 is 3
5 − 2 = 3

Skill: Recognizing the symbol −

page 116

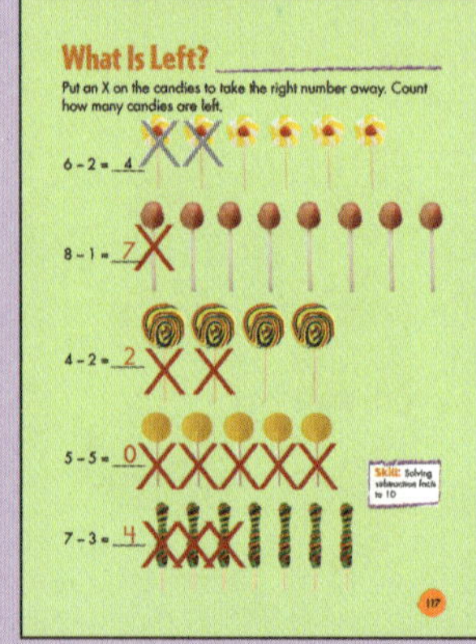
What Is Left?

Put an X on the candies to take the right number away. Count how many candies are left.

6 − 2 = 4

8 − 1 = 7

4 − 2 = 2

5 − 5 = 0

7 − 3 = 4

Skill: Solving subtraction facts to 10

page 117

Bye-Bye, Birdie

Count and write how many animals are in each set. Put an X on the animals you'd like to take away. Write that number. Count and write how many are left.

5 take away 2 is 3
5 − 2 = 3

8 − 4 = 4

6 − 3 = 3

5 − 2 = 3

5 − 1 = 4

4 − 2 = 2

Skill: Reviewing subtraction

page 118 page 119

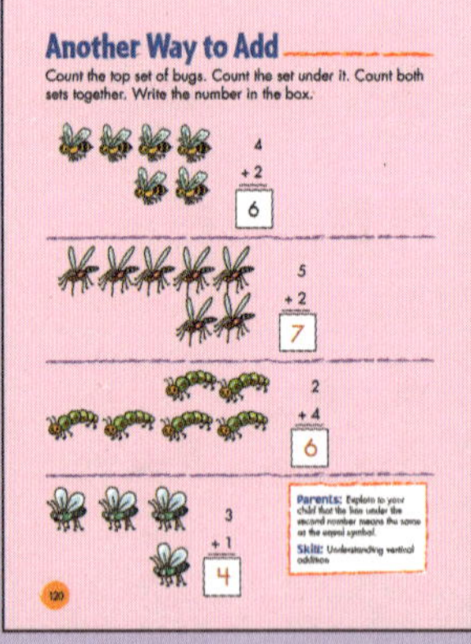
Another Way to Add

Count the top set of bugs. Count the set under it. Count both sets together. Write the number in the box.

4
+ 2
6

5
+ 2
7

2
+ 4
6

3
+ 1
4

Parents: Explain to your child that the line under the second number means the same as the equal symbol.

Skill: Understanding vertical addition

page 120

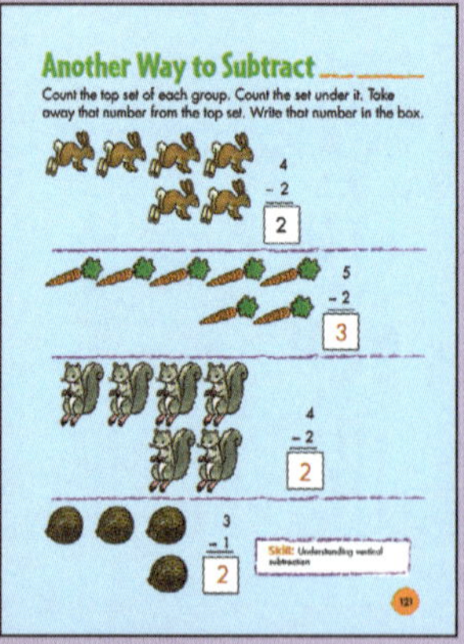
Another Way to Subtract

Count the top set of each group. Count the set under it. Take away that number from the top set. Write that number in the box.

4
− 2
2

5
− 2
3

4
− 2
2

3
− 1
2

Skill: Understanding vertical subtraction

page 121